IMAGES OF SPORT

NEATH RFC
1945–1996

IMAGES OF SPORT

NEATH RFC
1945-1996

MIKE PRICE

TEMPUS

First published 2004

Tempus Publishing Limited
The Mill, Brimscombe Port,
Stroud, Gloucestershire, GL5 2QG
www.tempus-publishing.com

British Library Cataloguing in Publication Data.
A catalogue record for this book is available from the British Library.

ISBN 0 7524 3106 4

Typesetting and origination by Tempus Publishing Limited.
Printed in Great Britain by Midway Colour Print, Wiltshire.

Contents

Acknowledgements

As with the first volume, once again I am indebted to the many people who have assisted with my search for items included in this publication.

Firstly, thanks are due to the Neath club itself for access to and use of its magnificent collection. The work of Ken Davies and Jim Giddings in compiling that collection has been invaluable – without their diligence, neither of these volumes would have been possible. Again, the staff at Neath and Swansea reference libraries have patiently put up with my requests for information.

In addition, I would like to thank David Richards of Rugby Relics, Malcolm Thomas, Dawn Thomas, Bill Davies, Rod Rees, Robert Scourfield, John Huins, Ceri Hopkins, Martyn Davies, Phil Pope, Glyn Davies and the host of other individuals who have contributed items.

Fay Harris of the *Neath Guardian* and David Evans of the *South Wales Evening Post* have again been most co-operative in allowing excerpts from their newspapers' groups pages to be reproduced.

If anything, this volume has been more difficult than the first if only due to the explosion in media interest in the last quarter of the century. Too much choice meant some tough decisions on what to omit! Although I have tried to avoid doing so, if I have in any way unintentionally infringed copyright anywhere, I apologise unreservedly and hope that any oversight will be forgiven as it is all in the interests of telling the tale of the Welsh All Blacks.

Finally, my thanks go to Becky Gadd and all at Tempus Publishing for their guidance and forbearance, especially Anthony Lovell during the final stages of production.

Introduction

This is the second 'Images of Sport' volume devoted to the development of Neath RFC. The earlier publication enveloped the period 1872 to 1945, from rugby's earliest beginnings at Neath through to the Second World War. This volume covers the period from 1945 to 1996 – from World War to professionalism.

When rugby football resumed in September 1945, Neath RFC already ranked firmly among the leading Welsh clubs. Little time was wasted in re-establishing that reputation as Tom James led Neath's heroic effort against the touring New Zealand Kiwis. In 1946/47 Neath became the first post-war Welsh champions; then Rees Stephens and Roy John became the club's first British Lions in 1950 and Courtenay Meredith built upon their formidable reputation for producing top-line forwards when he toured South Africa in 1955.

Forward power has been a constant theme throughout Neath's history. The late 1950s saw the emergence of Brian Thomas packing behind the mighty front row of Ron Waldron, Morlais Williams and John Dodd. It culminated in the Welsh championship being reclaimed in 1966/67, the season in which Dai Morris ('The Shadow') made his debut for Wales at the start of another 'golden era' for the Principality.

In 1971/72, Neath RFC became the first of the senior Welsh clubs to celebrate its centenary – 100 years after Dr T.P. Whittington and his pioneers had set the club on the course to fame. Neath celebrated in style, scrum-half Martyn Davies becoming the first club captain to hold aloft the Welsh Cup after a gripping 15-9 win over Llanelli in the first final of a competition that was to seize the imagination of the Welsh rugby public.

Neath's forward prowess has often led to their backs being overlooked, but Elgan Rees became the All Blacks' first behind-the-scrum Lion in 1977 and bettered it by becoming the club's first double Lion in 1980. The scene was set for what I call the

'Thomas Revolution', in which the incomparable Brian Thomas, assisted by Ron Waldron and Glen Ball, returned to The Gnoll to apply business principles to rugby in a most unique manner that launched the club on its path to unprecedented success.

Neath mirrored Brian's own uncompromising attitude to the game and the champagne flowed at The Gnoll as championships were won in 1986/87, 1988/89 and 1989/90, and back-to-back cup finals were won in 1988/89 and 1989/90. Players like Paul Thorburn, Jonathan Davies, Brian Williams, Kevin Phillips, Gareth Llewellyn and Allan Bateman (to name but a few) made their mark. Reigning world champions New Zealand, Australia and South Africa escaped by the skin of their teeth from The Gnoll. Neath won the first Welsh League title in 1990/91 and they won the first 'professional' title in 1995/96. Great years for a truly great club!

I have been extremely fortunate in knowing so many of these wonderful characters who have shaped post-war Neath rugby. From an early age, people like Rees Stephens, Ron Waldron, Brian Thomas and so many more coloured my rugby thinking. It has been a rare privilege to record here some of their deeds and to give the reader a flavour of their outstanding contribution to Welsh and indeed world rugby.

Mike Price
February 2004

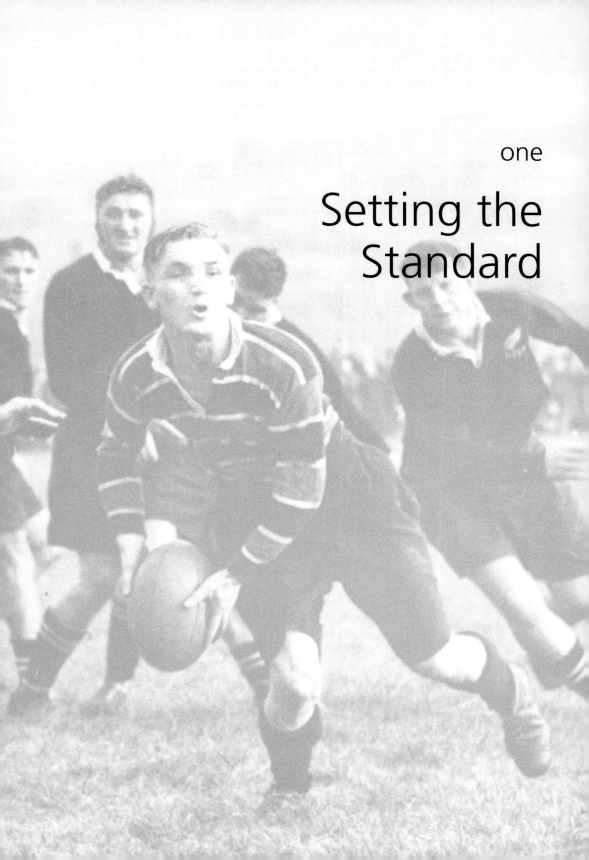

one

Setting the
Standard

Neath's first post-war captain was Tom James, a rock-hard back-rower from the Swansea Valley. Tom James first appeared for Neath in 1939 and was a true disciple of traditional Neath forward principles. His pre-match ritual involved removing his false teeth and rolling up his sleeves ready for action. Famously, he led the Welsh All Blacks against the New Zealand Kiwis and scored a try almost from the kick-off. He later played rugby league for Ystradgynlais when the thirteen-man code attempted one of its many breakthroughs into Wales.

NEW SET OF FAMOUS JERSEYS

By WANDERER

Thirty minutes from the kick-off of the Neath v. Cardiff game at the Gnoll this afternoon there was no doubt that the home club would have their expected good gate.

For the first time this season, the Neath followers could say they were watching the All Blacks in action, because the home club turned out in a new set of their famous jerseys. Teams:,

Neath.—D. Glyn Davies; Roy Williams, D. O'Sullivan, T. R. Davies (captain), M. Clement; A. Evans, J. R. Jones; Cliff Williams, L. Anthony, Les Davies, George Hughes, Graham Hughes, Rees Stephens, M. Thomas, H. Williams.

Cardiff.—St. John Rees; G. Jones, J. Matthias (captain), Bleddyn Williams, G. Hale; W, Darch, W. D. Cleaver; R. Bale, M. James, C. Davies, E. Morgan, Les Mansfield, H. E. Jones, W. E. Tamplin, A. McCarley.

Referee: Mr. Trevor Jones, Llangynwydd.

The game opened with each team taking the measure of the other, but a threequarter movement by Neath took them into the Cardiff 25, where play remained for some time.

Here Neath lost several scoring opportunities, one when T. R. Davies failed with a penalty kick. St. John Rees was sound at full-back for Cardiff, and his efforts did much to prevent Neath from crossing his line.

Play became exceptionally mediocre and, apart from a catastrophic tearing of one of Neath's new jerseys, there was nothing in the game to arouse the enthusiasm of the large crowd.

BLACKS SCORE

D. Glyn Davies, who, like St. John Rees, was making some grand clearances, sent the ball into the touch-line near the visitors' goal, and from a melee which followed the line-out REES STEPHENS crossed to give the All Blacks the lead. Davies could not complete his good work by adding the extra points.

Stephens was injured while going over the line and had to leave the field for five minutes.

Two excellent Cardiff three-quarter movements were spoiled by faulty handling, but the third, started by Matthews, ended in BLEDDYN WILLIAMS touching down for a try which St. John Rees converted.

Half-time Score:

NEATH—1 try (3pts.).
CARDIFF—1 con. goal (5pts.).

SECOND HALF

Early in the second half TAMPLIN scored a penalty goal for Cardiff, and J. R. JONES shortly afterwards reduced the lead by scoring Neath's second try.

Five minutes before the end HALE scored a try for Cardiff and J. R. Jones kicked a penalty goal for Neath at the last minute.

Final:
Neath 1 pen. goal, 2 tries, 9pts.
Cardiff 1 con. goal, 1 pen. goal, 1 try. 11pts.

After losing a warm-up game against Glynneath, Neath's first big post-war fixture was against Cardiff. Rees Stephens debuted for Neath against the star-studded visitors who were led by centre Jack Matthews. Matthews and Bleddyn Williams had played pre-war for Neath, and Cardiff also included Neath's international flanker Alan McCarley who was elected skipper of the All Blacks in 1939/40.

Neath gradually regrouped and this XV took on and so nearly beat the 1945 N.Z. Army side, or Kiwis, as they were known. The Neath XV wore Glamorgan County colours so as to avoid a clash with the tourists' all black. Second-row Graham Hughes, Rees Stephens and Morlais Thomas all appeared for Wales in Victory Internationals in 1945/46. From left to right, standing: G. Goldsworthy (Referee), L. Anthony, M. Thomas, S.F. Simmonds (Chairman), C. Williams, T.H. Bevan, Graham Hughes, J.R.G. Stephens, George Hughes, D.J. Davies (Trainer). Seated: R. Williams, D.G. Davies, T. James (Captain), T.D. James, J. Thomas, K. Hardwick. Front: H. Parker, W.E. Jones.

Action from the Kiwis game. Scrum-half Harold Parker launches a Neath attack close to the New Zealand line. Tom James and Rees Stephens look on.

NEATH'S GOOD GAME AGAINST N. ZEALANDERS

By WANDERER

Neath—15 pts ; New Zealand Tourists—22 pts.

If the result of a Rugby game depended on the amount of time that a team spends in its opponents' 25, then Neath would have emerged as victors from the game with the Kiwis at the Gnoll on Saturday.

The Kiwis won because they were exceptionally heavier and faster, and took good advantage of the opportunities given them.

As in the Swansea game, the New Zealanders were soon in arrears, Tom James touching down within four minutes of the kick-off. From that moment the 12,000 spectators were kept on their toes as they witnessed a game of thrills and excitement.

It was the New Zealand men, trained soldiers, not working lads, who first began to tire. For the greater part of the second half the Dominion fifteen were on the defence, Neath gallantly keeping up the pressure until the final whistle.

PERFECT RUGBY

The one thing which will remain in the minds of those who saw the game will be the mighty performance of the Neath pack. The Kiwi forwards never attained the heights reached by the Welshmen who played with a perfection rarely seen in modern Rugby. The New Zealanders, after the game, acknowledged the fine work of the Neath pack.

The "star" man of the Neath team was W. E. Jones, making his first appearance since the war. He proved that the trouble experienced by the club in getting him released from R.A.F. duties had been well worth while.

Parker, at inside-half, proved worthy of his first appearance in the side.

W. E. Jones scored nine of Neath's 15 points, with a try and two penalty goals. Two unconverted tries were touched down by Tom James and T. D. James.

The *South Wales Evening Post* match report as penned by Wally Thomas, alias 'Wanderer' who was to cover Neath's exploits for forty years for various newspapers in the locality.

NEATH RUGBY FOOTBALL CLUB

SEASON 1945/46 — **CAPTAIN - TOM JAMES**

Sept.	1	Glynneath	L	0	3	H
	8	Open				A
	15	Llanelly				A
	22	Cardiff	L	9	11	H
	29	Briton Ferry	W	26	3	A
Oct.	6	Llanelly	W	15	3	H
	13	Newport	L	11	22	A
	20	Briton Ferry	W	11	0	H
	27	Pontypool	W	8	7	H
Nov.	3	New Zealand Kiwis	L	15	22	H
	10	Amman United	W	9	3	A
	17	Open				
	24	Swansea	C			A
Dec.	1	Gloucester	L	5	6	A
	1	*Welsh Trial Reds v Whites (Cardiff)*				
	8	Newport	W	14	13	H
	15	Penarth	W	25	0	A
	22	Bristol	L	0	5	A
	25	London Welsh	W	9	0	H
	26	Abertillery	W	12	5	H
	29	Pontypool	W	9	3	A
Jan.	5	Llanelly	C			H
	5	*WALES 3 pts NEW ZEALAND KIWIS 11 pts*				
	12	Newbridge	W	8	0	H
	19	*ENGLAND 25 pts WALES 13 pts*				
	26	Cardiff	L	5	8	A
Feb.	2	*SCOTLAND 26 pts WALES 5 pts*				
	9	Bridgend	W	39	0	H
	11	Welsh Guards	W	28	3	H
	16	Llanelly	W	25	9	H
	23	Swansea	W	19	8	H
Mar.	2	*Aberavon v N.Z. Kiwis*				
	9	*WALES 6 pts IRELAND 4 pts*				
	16	Gloucester	W	9	8	H
	19	Llanelly	W	3	0	H
	23	Bristol	W	13	5	H
	28	Aberavon	W	4	0	A
	30	Newbridge	W	18	3	A
	30	*WALES 11 pts SCOTLAND 13 pts*				
Apr.	6	Swansea	W	6	0	H
	11	Aberavon	W	17	6	H
	13	Bridgend	W	16	4	A
	20	Abertillery	W	5	0	A
	25	Glyn Stephens' Welsh XV	W	19	3	H
	27	Glynneath	W	6	5	A
May	2	Ystradgynlais	W	20	11	A

Left: Neath RFC results from the first post-war 'season' 1945/46.

Opposite below: The Reds XV in the first post-war Welsh trial played on 1 December 1945 at a bomb-damaged Cardiff Arms Park. Neath had two representatives in hooker Cliff Williams and lock Rees Stephens. D. Glyn Davies, Graham Bevan and Tom James appeared for the Whites. From left to right, standing: E. Jones (Swansea), W.E. Tamplin (Cardiff), G. Bevan (Llanelly), E. Gwyther (Llanelly), Cliff Williams (Neath), A.D. Allen (Penygraig), J.R.G. Stephens (Neath), T. Jones (Referee). Seated: W.E. Williams (Newport), L. Williams (Llanelly), B.L. Williams (Cardiff), P. Rees (Llanelly), R.H. Lloyd-Davies (London Welsh), J. Maiden (Newbridge). Front: W. Darch (Cardiff), W.B. Cleaver (Cardiff).

Above: Neath RFC 1945/46: Played 36, Won 28, Drawn 0, Lost 8, Points For 469, Points Against 168. From left to right, back row: B. Sutcliffe, R. Jenkins, T. Rouse, J. John, J.T. Evans. Standing: J. Rowlands, L. Anthony, H. Williams, L. Davies, G. Hughes, T.H. Bevan, J.R.G. Stephens, D.G. Swain, T. Rees, R. Williams. Seated: J. Williams, J.W.D. Jenkins, V. Evans, C. Williams, S.F. Simmons (Chairman), T. James (Captain), A.E. Freethy (Secretary), C. Challinor, M. Thomas, J. Thomas. Front: E. Davies, H. Parker, P. James, T. Davies.

Wales *v.* England, 19 January 1946. England won this Victory International (for which no caps were awarded) 25-13. Two Neath players figured for the Reds: Rees Stephens (who went on to win 32 caps) and Graham Hughes, who sadly was never capped. From left to right, standing: E. Jones (Swansea), G. Bevan (Llanelly), A. Brickell (Abertillery), W.E. Tamplin (Cardiff), G. Hughes (Neath), J.R.G. Stephens (Neath), W.G. Jones (Newport), I. Jones (Touch Judge). Seated: L. Williams (Llanelly), J. Matthews (Cardiff), L. Manfield (Cardiff, Captain), B.L. Williams (Cardiff), G. Hale (Cardiff), R.H. Lloyd-Davies (London Welsh). Front: W. Davies (Cardiff University), G. Davies (Pontypridd).

Hughes and Stephens bear down on the unfortunate England scrum-half.

SCOTLAND		WALES	
Full Back	K. I. GEDDES (Capt.) 15 *London Scottish*	(A) R. LLOYD DAVIES ... Full Back *London Welsh*	
Right Wing	C. W. DRUMMOND 14 *Melrose*	(E) W. E. WILLIAMS ... Left Wing *Newport*	
Right Centre	W. H. MUNRO 13 *Glasgow H.S.F.P. and Army*	(D) BLEDDYN WILLIAMS Left Centre *Cardiff*	
Left Centre	C. R. BRUCE 12 *Glasgow Acads. and Army*	(C) JACK MATTHEWS Right Centre *Cardiff (Capt.)*	
Left Wing	D. W. C. SMITH 11 *Aberdeen Univ.*	(B) LESLIE WILLIAMS Right Wing *Llanelly and Devon Services*	
Outside Half	I. J. M. LUMSDEN 10 *Watsonians*	(F) GLYN DAVIES ... Outside Half *Pontypridd County School*	
Scrum Half	A. W. BLACK 9 *Edinburgh University*	(G) WYNFORD DAVIES Scrum Half *Cardiff University and Pontypridd C.S.*	

REFEREE
Mr. H. L. V. DAY
Rugby Union (Leicester)

Any last-minute changes will be
notified on board sent around the
field.

Touch Judges
Scotland—Mr. F. J. C. Moffat (S.R.U.)
Wales—Mr. Ifor Jones (Gorseinon)

Music to-day by the famous
Gwauncaegurwen Prize Band
Conducted by Mr. David Lloyd

Forwards:		Forwards:	
8 J. H. ORR ... Heriot's F.P.		(H) LES MANFIELD ... Cardiff	
7 D. W. DEAS ... Heriot's F.P.		(I) REES STEPHENS ... Neath	
6 W. I. D. ELLIOTT ... Academical-Wdrs.		(J) D. H. STEER Abercarn and Taunton	
5 J. KIRK ... Academical-Wdrs.		(K) GRAHAM HUGHES ... Neath	
4 A. G. M. WATT ... Academical-Wdrs.		(L) RAY HUGHES ... Aberavon	
3 R. AITKEN ... London Scottish		(M) F. E. MORRIS Pill H. and Newport	
2 G. LYALL ... Gala		(N) MALDWYN JAMES ... Cardiff	
1 I. C. HENDERSON Academical-Wdrs.		(O) GRIFF BEVAN ... Llanelly	

The programme from the Victory International against Scotland at Cardiff Arms Park on 30 March 1946 when Wales, including Rees Stephens and Graham Hughes, lost 11–13.

Menu card from a celebratory dinner held in May 1946 to mark fifty years of unbroken service by Walter E. Rees as secretary of the WRU.

Cliff Williams took over the captaincy in 1946/47. Like Tom James, he too was an Ystradgynlais product, and he was an inspirational choice, for he led Neath to the first post-war Welsh championship. Cliff Williams had first appeared for the All Blacks in 1939. He never received higher honours but his value to Neath was considerable. Neath has always been fortunate in having a string of quality hookers, all utterly dependable men. Neath fans consider it a travesty that the likes of Ray Jenkins, Morlais Williams, Norman Rees and Mike Richards never earned the ultimate reward of a Welsh cap.

Neath RFC 1946/47: Welsh Champions for the sixth time. The All Blacks won the first post-war Welsh championship in 1946/47. Their record was: Played 40, Won 32, Drew 4, Lost 4, Points For 502, Points Against 163. From left to right, back row: S.F. Simmons, J. Shufflebotham, H. Williams, J. Thomas, V. Friend, L. Anthony, D.G. Swain, J. Rouse (Committee), J. Williams (Committee), R. Parker (Baggage man). Middle row: J.T. Evans (Committee), C. Challinor, T. Randall, T.H. Bevan, T. James, L. Davies, J.R.G. Stephens, E.R. John, B. Sutcliffe (Treasurer), M. John (Chairman). Front row: M. Thomas, H.O. Edwards, A.E. Freethy (Secretary), C. Williams (Captain), J.W.D. Jenkins (Vice Captain), T. Davies (Treasurer), V. Evans, A. Duenas, R. Jenkins (Vice Chairman), D.J. Davies (Trainer).

NEATH RUGBY FOOTBALL CLUB

SEASON 1946/47   CAPTAIN - CLIFF WILLIAMS

Sept.	7 Crynant	W	22	0	H	
	12 Briton Ferry	W	23	3	A	
	14 Bridgend	W	12	0	H	
	21 Cardiff	W	14	8	H	
	28 Aberavon	L	12	13	H	
Oct.	5 Llanelly	L	7	11	A	
	12 Leicester	D	6	6	A	
	14 Guy's Hospital	W	26	5	H	
	19 Cross Keys	W	17	3	H	
	24 Glynneath	D	8	8	A	
	26 Pontypool	W	15	11	H	
Nov.	2 St. Mary's Hospital	W	12	6	A	
	4 Guy's Hospital	W	28	3	A	
	9 Swansea	W	12	3	H	a
	16 Bridgend	W	3	0	A	
	23 Aberavon	C			H	
	30 Newbridge	D	6	6	A	
Dec.	7 Llanelly	W	7	3	H	
	14 Devonport Services	W	22	0	H	
	21 Maesteg	C			A	
	25 London Welsh				H	
	26 Aberavon	W	10	0	A	
	28 Abertillery	W	4	3	H	
Jan.	4 Llanelly	L	3	4	A	
	11 Newbridge	W	6	5	H	
	13 Exeter	W	18	0	H	
	18 *WALES 6 pts ENGLAND 9 pts*					
	25 Cardiff	D	3	3	A	
Feb.	1 *SCOTLAND 8 pts WALES 22 pts*					
	1 London Welsh	C			A	
	8 Penarth	C			H	
	13 Newport	C			A	
	15 Cheltenham	C			H	
	17 Cross Keys	C			A	
	22 Llanelly	C			H	
Mar.	1 Swansea	W	9	3	A	
	8 *WALES v IRELAND (postponed)*					
	13 Aberavon	W	3	0	H	
	15 Penarth	C			A	
	22 *FRANCE nil WALES 3 pts*					
	22 Bristol	W	13	3	A	
	27 Glynneath	W	27	0	H	
	29 *WALES 6 pts IRELAND nil*					
	29 Pontypool	W	11	0	A	
Apr.	5 Maesteg (abandoned - 55 minutes)	C				
	7 Aberavon	W	20	3	H	
	12 Abertillery	W	18	0	H	
	19 Newport	W	15	0	H	
	21 Penclawdd	W	15	3	A	b
	26 Devonport Services	W	26	8	A	
	28 Exeter	W	11	3	A	
May	3 Newport	W	12	11	A	
	5 Cross Keys	W	10	3	A	
	10 Llanelly	W	9	7	H	
	12 Maesteg	L	3	4	A	

a	J.W.D.Jenkins scored all 4 tries
b	E.R. John debut
*	J.R.G. Stephens played in all 4 Wales internationals
	T.H.Bevan, D.G.Swain, Viv Evans, H.O.Edwards, J.W.D.Jenkins, Les Davies played in trials

Neath RFC results 1946/47 – the first post-war championship and Neath's fifth in all.

NEATH
UNOFFICIAL
CHAMPIONS

Neath, *1-2-9; Llanelly, 12-0-7
*Penalty: One penalty, one dropped
Attendance. 12,000.

NEATH proved themselves worthy champions of the unofficial Welsh Rugby Union and retained their ground record when they defeated Llanelly by nine points to seven at the Gnoll, Neath.

The Neath victory was more decisive than the score suggests, for they outplayed the Scarlets in all phases of the game and the issue rarely looked in doubt.

Neath played as they have been playing all the season as a team, and are without question one of the soundest sides in the country. In view of this teamwork it would be unfair to single out any one player for praise, but credit must be given to the Neath captain and hooker, Cliff Williams, who is retiring from the game after the last match against Maesteg to-day. This veteran forward, has held the pack together and hooked consistently well—on Saturday he got the ball back from the scrummages 34 times as against Jeffrey's 16. He will be missed in Neath pack next year.

For Llanelly Ron Williams, fly-half, Jim Davies, full-back, and Griff Bevan, in the pack, did all that could be expected of them, but these three alone could not top the victory march of the "All Blacks."

PENALTY GOALS

Much against the run of the play. Llanelly scored first, when Griff Bevan landed a good penalty goal from 35 yards out in the 25th minute. Within 10 minutes Neath drew level when Tom Randall with a grand kick converted a penalty.

The sides crossed over on level terms, but the hammering the Llanelly pack had taken in the loose during the first session was soon evident and in the 49th minute, John Jenkins, a strong running wing three-quarter, dashed over in the corner, after receiving from John Thomas, for an unconverted try. Two minutes later a delightful passing movement, in which forwards and backs took part, culminated in the long-legged flyer, Horace Edwards, scoring a picture try near the corner flag. Tom Randall failed to goal.

Llanelly soon revealed that they had a sting in their tail when Ron Lewis dropped a goal four minutes from the end.

Following the final whistle cup final scenes were enacted and thousands of spectators invaded the field to congratulate the first post-war Rugby champions. Neath's record at the top of the unofficial table now reads: Played 39, won 31, lost 3, drawn 5, 531pts. for 151 against.

Cartoonist 'Pell' made the most of Neath's triumph.

Neath clinched the championship by beating Llanelly at The Gnoll.

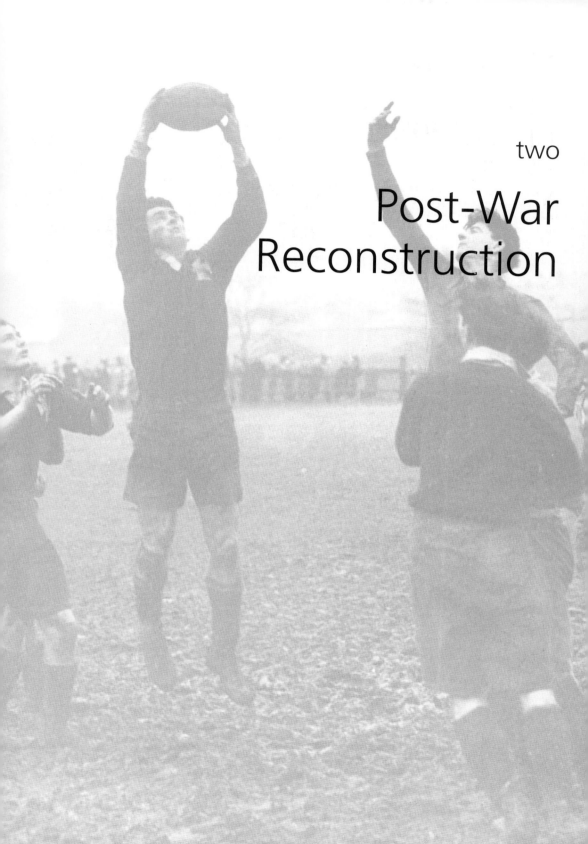

two

Post-War
Reconstruction

Above, below and opposite above: Three action shots from the Neath & Aberavon combined XV *v.* Australia at The Gnoll on 25 October 1947. The Wallabies triumphed 19–9, the home side's points coming from a try by Aberavon's Emlyn Davies and two penalties by Neath's Granville Jones, but Neath (the reigning Welsh Champions) were not impressed by the compromise selection of the combined XV that omitted their championship-winning front five.

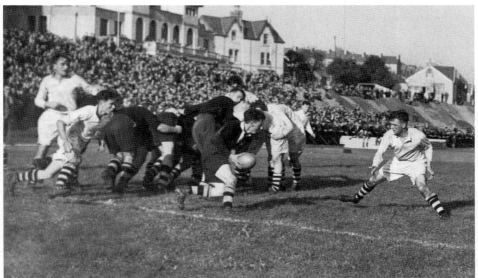

Swansea *v.* Neath, October 1948. All Blacks scrum–half Frank Williams (later an Aberavon committeeman) attempts to break away from a scrum. Note the packed terrace in front of the old St Helen's Pavilion.

Opposite above: Thanks to the influence of treasurer Theo Davies, The Gnoll frequently hosted county games and this programme was produced for the Glamorgan game against Pembrokeshire in November 1947. Glamorgan won 24-0.

Opposite below: Les Anthony, another hardened forward from the Swansea Valley school, was capped in 1948. The Cwmllynfell-reared prop wore the jersey lettered J when Wales played Scotland at Cardiff on Saturday 7 February 1948.

Right: Rees Stephens wins line-out ball for Neath — and they complain about playing surfaces today!

Above: Full-back Viv Evans captained Neath in 1947/48.

Neath RFC season ticket from 1947/48.

DATE	Fixture List 1947-48 OPPONENTS	Ground	Result	SCORE					
				Neath			Opponents		
1947				G	T	P	G	T.	P
Sept. 6	Resolven	Home							
,, 13	Maesteg	Home							
,, 18	Skewen (Thursday) ...	Away							
,, 20	Penarth	Home							
,, 27	Bridgend	Home							
Oct. 4	Llanelly	Home							
,, 11	Leicester ...	Home							
,, 18	Cheltenham	Away							
,, 25	Neath & Aberavon v. Australians	Home							
,, 30	St. Mary's H'sptl. (Thurs)	Home							
Nov. 1	Resolven	Away							
,, 8	Swansea	Away							
,, 15	Bridgend	Away							
,, 22	Pontypool ...	Home							
,, 29	Newbridge	Home							
Dec. 6	Llanelly	Away							
,, 13	Newport	Away							
,, 20	Abertillery ...	Away							
,, 25	London Welsh (Xmas D.)	Home							
,, 26	Aberavon (Boxing Day)	Home							
,, 27	Penarth	Away							
1948									
Jan. 3	Cardiff	Away							
,, 10	Cheltenham ...	Home							
,, 17	England v. Wales	Twickenham							
,, 17	Cross Keys ...	Away							
,, 24	Cardiff ...	Home							
,, 31	London Welsh ...	Away							
Feb. 2	Guy's Hospital ...	Away							
,, 7	Wales v. Scotland	Cardiff							
,, 14	Llanelly	Home							
,, 21	Wales v. France ...	Swansea							
,, 23	Guy's Hospital ...	Home							
,, 28	Maesteg	Away							
Mar. 6	Pontypool	Away							
,, 13	Newbridge	Away							
,, 13	Wales v. Ireland ...	Belfast							
,, 20	Swansea	Home							
,, 27	Cross Keys ...	Home							
,, 29	Aberavon (Easter Mon.)	Away							
April 3	Abertillery	Home							
,, 10	Llanelly	Away							
,, 17	Newport	Home							
,, 24	Possible French Tour ..	Open							

Programme from the Neath *v.* Cardiff match played at The Gnoll on Saturday 24 January 1948. Cardiff lost only two games in 1947/48 (to Pontypool and Penarth) but Neath, the reigning champions, took them close twice, losing this one 5–6 and three weeks earlier 0–3 at the Arms Park.

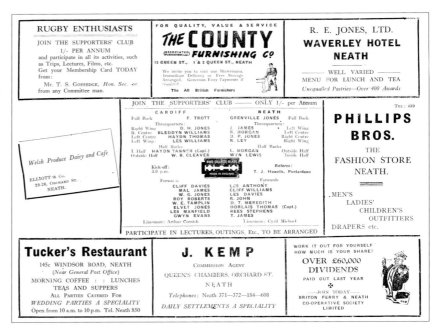

Neath RFC 1947/48: Played 40, Won 29, Drawn 2, Lost 9, Points For 446, Points Against 175. Neath started the defence of their title strongly and in a friendly against local club Skewen registered a record 66–0 win, but, wrote J.B.G. Thomas, the absence of internationals Stephens and Anthony disrupted their challenge. From left to right, back row: W.A. Griffiths (Committee), C.F. Michael (Committee), S.T. Simmons (Committee), J. Shufflebotham (Committee), R. Ley, A. Trotman, L. Anthony, D.T. Meredith, J. Rouse, J. Williams, C. Challinor, R. Parker. Standing: V. Friend (Committee), T. Lodge (Committee), D.R. Morgan, T. Randall, T.H. Bevan, T. James, L. Davies, J.R.G. Stephens, E.R. John, I. Evans, W.D. Smith, M. John (Committee). Seated: M. Thomas, H.O. Edwards, A.E. Freethy (Secretary), V. Evans (Captain), C. Williams, R. Jenkins (Chairman), B. Sutcliffe, T. Davies (Treasurer), J.W.D. Jenkins, A. Duenas, D.J. Davies (Trainer). Front row: T.A. Shufflebotham, W. Lewis, L. Morgan, J. James, W. Davies.

A programme of note – Penarth v. Neath, 5 February 1949. Centre Lewis Jones equalled the club's match-scoring record that day with 18 points (3 tries, 3 conversions and a penalty). Gorseinon-product Jones enjoyed a brilliant career. He became the first-ever player to fly out to join the Lions as a replacement when he went to New Zealand

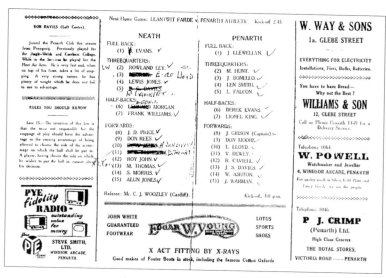

in 1950 and won caps for Wales from Devonport Services and Llanelly. He then joined Leeds Rugby League and set numerous records in that code too. A late change brought winger Roy Lambert into the Neath side and he went on to represent Wales at rugby league too.

Back-row forward Morlais Thomas led Neath in 1948/49 when they achieved a modest fifty per cent record, which read: Played 42, Won 19, Drew 4, and Lost 19, Points For 369, Points Against 303. From left to right, back row: F. Squires, T. Rouse, S.F. Simmons, J. Shufflebotham, R. Jenkins, A.R. Harris (all Committee). Standing: M. Johns (Committee), J.D. Price, D.T. Meredith, J.R.G. Stephens, E.R. John, J. Sullivan, L. Morgan, C.F. Michael (Committee). Seated: D.R. Morgan, V. Evans, W.A. Griffiths (Assistant Secretary), A.E. Freethy (Secretary), M. Thomas (Captain), B. Sutcliffe (Chairman), T. Davies (Treasurer), T.J. Griffiths, Dr A. Jones. Front: G. Jones (Trainer), E. Rees, F. Williams, R. Ley, K. Maddocks, R. Parker (Assistant Trainer).

Horace Edwards captained Neath in 1949/50. A most accomplished centre, Edwards originally played for Cardiff before the Second World War and was chosen for Wales against Ireland only for the match to be postponed. He joined Neath for their 'missing' season of 1939/40 when he was included in the Welsh team that played Red Cross internationals against England.

The Neath XV that defeated Pontypool 3-0 at The Gnoll, 24 February 1950. From left to right, standing: W. Millett (Touch Judge), J. Thorley, J. Harris, G. Lewis, R. Jenkins, N. Edwards, J. Jones, J.R.G. Stephens, G. Jones (Trainer). Seated: E. Thomas, H. Hopkins, E.R. John (Captain), V. Evans, D. Bater, E. Jones, J. Huins, R. Morgan.

three

The Stephens
and John Years

The playing careers of two Neath and Wales greats coincided just after the Second World War. Rees Stephens *(above left)* and Roy John *(above centre)* came to characterise all that is best about Neath rugby with their distinguished contribution to Welsh forward play. The pair became Neath's first Lions (R.K. Green had toured New Zealand with the Anglo-Welsh XV of 1908) and represented Wales together on 12 occasions. They carried the name of Neath high to all corners of the rugby world and could truly be said to be world-class forwards. Stephens won 32 caps for Wales between 1947 and 1957, Roy John won 19 between 1950 and 1954. Stephens, a real fitness fanatic, was usually to be seen with socks around his ankles providing the uncompromising hard graft for every side he played in. 'King John' returned from the 1950 Lions tour acclaimed as the greatest exponent of line-out play in the world. His towering leap is said to have allowed him to clap his hands *above* The Gnoll crossbar and such were his footballing skills that he even did duty at centre and full-back now and again.

Above right: Of the many distinguished All Blacks, few can have contributed as much to Neath rugby as Rees Stephens. Rees, the son of former Neath forward and Wales captain Glyn Stephens, was always destined for high rugby honours. Educated locally at Alderman Davies' School, then Llandovery College, he represented Welsh Schools for two years in 1934/35 and 1935/36, and spent the war years employed in his father's coal mines. He first appeared for Neath against Cardiff on 16 September 1945 and soon won a place in the Welsh XV that contested Victory Internationals in 1945/46. He won the first of his 32 Welsh caps (then a record for a Welsh forward) against England in 1947 and his last against France in 1957. A Barbarian, together with Roy John, he toured Australasia with the 1950 Lions and was greatly impressed by the Otago style of rucking which he quickly imported to Neath. He captained the club for three seasons, 1951/52, 1952/53 and 1953/54, and later became a committeeman and trustee as well as a Welsh selector during the 'golden era'. Something of a rugby visionary, Rees Stephens was also instrumental in setting up Neath Colts/Neath Athletic RFC, a source of over 300 post-war players for the senior club, of which he was chairman until his death in 1999.

Opposite above: The 1950 British Lions tour party. From left to right, back row: G.M. Budge, J.D. Robins, R. Macdonald, J.S. McCarthy, M.F. Lane, D.M. Davies, V.G. Roberts, M.C. Thomas, T. Clifford. Standing: D.W.C. Smith, G.W. Norton, J.E. Nelson, D.J. Hayward, J.R.G. Stephens, E.R. John, R.T. Evans, J.W. McKay, N.J. Henderson, K.J. Jones. Sitting: W.B. Cleaver, P.W. Kininmonth, B.L. Williams (Vice-Captain), L.B. Osborne (Manager), K.D. Mullen (Captain), E.L. Savage (Secretary), I. Preece, C. Davies, J. Matthews. Front: A.W. Black, J.W. Kyle, W.R. Willis, G. Rimmer. Inset: B.L. Jones.

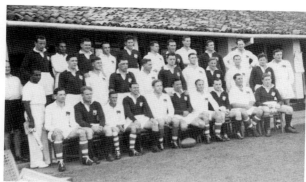

Left: On their way home by sea, the 1950 Lions stopped off at Ceylon (now Sri Lanka) and played an exhibition game at Colombo Racecourse against the national XV. Rees Stephens and Roy John are pictured in the middle row and a Ceylon jersey given to Roy John adorns The Gnoll clubhouse today.

Below: Action shot from the above game played on 18 September 1950.

Those Lions tours of far-off days were much more fun than the modern jet-propelled trips. Here, the Neath pair show off some distinctly local headgear.

Roy John seems to be enjoying the attentions of a local reptile – if he got into difficulties he could probably have leaped further than the snake could strike anyway!

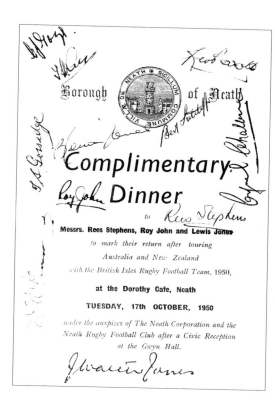

Left: Neath rarely need a reason to celebrate and the old Neath Borough Council staged a dinner to mark the return of Rees Stephens.

Below: Roy John and Lewis Jones from the Lions tour in 1950. Following their return from the Lions tour, Stephens and John were in great demand to appear for many select teams. In November 1950 they joined many of their Lions team-mates in Major R.V. Stanley's XV at Oxford University. From left to right, standing: J.S. McCarthy, C.L. Griffith, C. Davies, M. Walker, R. MacDonald, G.L. Bullard, M.F. Lane, W.J. Hefer, E.R. John (Neath), M.B. Hofmeyr, R. Willis. Standing: R.E. Prescott (Touch Judge), D. Lewis, T. Clifford, B. Boobyer, V.G. Roberts, C.E. Winn, M.C. Thomas, G.C. Rittson-Thomas, J.R.G. Stephens (Neath), D.A. Emms, G.R. Rimmer, H.A. Fry (Referee), J. Northcote-Green (Touch Judge). Seated: L.B. Cannell, Dr J. Matthews, H.D. Small, K.D. Mullen, J.MacG. Kendall-Carpenter (Captain), Major R.V. Stanley, P.W. Kininmonth (Captain), R. Green, B.L. Williams, I.J. Botting.

Neath RFC, skippered by Roy John, pictured prior to their game at Bristol on 28 April 1951. From left to right, standing: M. John (Committee), A.E. Freethy (Committee), T. Davies (Committee), E. Thomas (later to captain Cardiff RFC), J. Thorley, J.R.G. Stephens, C.C. Meredith, L. Harris, G. Lewis, G. Wells, N. Edwards, R. Jenkins, S. Davies (Committee), W.R. Millett (Committee). Kneeling: G. Thomas, J. Huins, E.R. John (Captain), V. Evans, D. Thomas, E. Jones.

The classic line-out skill of Roy John is captured in this game against Llanelly. Note the organisational excellence ('blocking') of his fellow Neath forwards that allowed him to jump unimpeded.

Neath RFC 1951/52 pictured in front of a full house in the old grandstand. From left to right, back row: R. Jenkins, W. Brennan, K. Maddocks. Standing: W. Millett (Touch Judge), G. Wells, G. Lewis, L. Harris, E.R. John, J. Thorley, -?-, A. Pritchard (Referee), G. Jones (Trainer). Seated: E. Jones, G. Thomas, V. Evans, J.R.G. Stephens (Captain), C.C. Meredith, E. Thomas, J. Huins. Front row: E. Jones, D. Thomas, D. Bater.

Neath won 15-11 against Swansea at St Helen's on 29 September 1951. From left to right, standing: T.H. Phillips (Referee), N. Edwards, G. Lewis, G. Wells, R. Jenkins, L. Harris, E. Thomas, K. Maddocks, C.C. Meredith. Seated: E. Jones, J. Thorley, D. Thomas, J.R.G. Stephens (Captain), V. Evans, Elvet Jones, G. Thomas.

Stephens and John were regular members of the Barbarians' Easter touring party. This is the 1952 group pictured at Cardiff Arms Park. From left to right, back row: G.E. Jones, F.D. Sykes, F.G. Griffiths, R. Bazley, I. King, M.C. Thomas, J.D. Robins, E.M.P. Hardy, J.H. Smith, R. Roe, P. Kavanagh, R. Kavanagh. Standing: J.P. Jordan, D.R. Gent, D.T. Wilkins, W.C. Woodgate, M.J. Berridge, J.E. Nelson, J.R.G. Stephens (Neath), E.R. John (Neath), S.J. Adkins, A. Forward, B.M. Gray, R.C.C. Thomas, O.L. Owen. Seated: D. Marsden-Jones, T. Wallace, W.E. Crawford, H. Waddell, H.L.G. Hughes, H.A. Haigh-Smith, M.R. Steele-Bodger, C.R. Hopwood, V.G.J. Jenkins, A. Wemyss. Front row: J.H. Henderson, D.M. Davies, D.W. Shuttleworth, M. Regan, K.M. Spence, J. Butterfield.

THE TEAMS

BARBARIANS				SOUTH AFRICA	
Touch Judge : Mr. M. R. STEELE-BODGER (England)		Full Backs		Touch Judge : B. S. VIVIERS (Orange Free State)	
16 G. WILLIAMS	Llanelly and Wales			J. BUCHLER (1) or A. C. KEEVY (2)	
				Transvaal Eastern Transvaal	
		Three-Quarters			
15 J. E. WOODWARD	Wasps and England	R. Wing	L. Wing	J. K. OCHSE	Western Province 3
14 L. B. CANNELL	St. Mary's Hos. and England	R. Centre	L. Centre	M. T. LATEGAN	Western Province 8
12 B. L. WILLIAMS (Vice-Capt.)	...Cardiff & Wales	L. Centre	R. Centre	R. VAN SCHOOR	Rhodesia 7
11 KEN JONES	Newport and Wales	L. Wing	R. Wing	P. JOHNSTONE (6) or F. MARAIS (4)	
				Western Province Boland	
		Halves			
10 CLIFF MORGAN	Cardiff and Wales	Outside	Outside	J. D. BREWIS N. Trans.(11) or P. JOHNSTONE	
9 W. R. WILLIS	Cardiff and Wales	Inside	Inside	P. A DU TOIT ... N. Transvaal (Vice-Capt.) 15	
		Forwards			
8 R. V. STIRLING	R.A.F. and England			F. E. VAN der RYST	Transvaal 19
7 D. M. DAVIES	...Somerset Pol. and Wales			W. DELPORT	Eastern Province 17
6 J. KENDALL CARPENTER	...Penzance and England			H. BEKKER	... N. Transvaal 21
5 ROY JOHN	Neath and Wales			E. DINKELMANN	...N. Transvaal 24
4 J. E. NELSON (Capt.)	...Malone and Ireland			J. DU RAND	, Rhodesia 29
3 V. G. ROBERTS	...Harlequins and England			S. P. FRY	Western Province 27
2 REES STEPHENS	Neath and Wales			H. MULLER (Capt.)	Transvaal 31
1 W. I. D. ELLIOTT	Edin. Acad. and Scotland			C. J. VAN WYK	Transvaal 26

Reserves: M. C. THOMAS (Wales), D. SHUTTLEWORTH (England) and W. A. HOLMES (England)

Referee :
Captain M. J. DOWLING (Ireland)
Kick-off 2.45 p.m.

On Saturday 26 January 1952, Stephens and John appeared for the Barbarians in their first-ever clash with the Springboks at Cardiff.

The match programme from the final game of the 1951/52 season,
a 17-10 home win over Newport that was achieved via 4 tries by
John Thorley, Morwyn Morgan, John Huins and Denzil Thomas and
featured a monster touchline penalty goal by Rees Stephens.

Neath RFC 1952/53. From left to right, back: R. Waldron, C.C. Meredith, B. Sparkes. Standing:
R. Parker (Trainer), R. Jenkins, G. Lewis, G. Evans, E.R. John, D. Devereux, T. Thomas,
H. Branch, G. Jones (Trainer). Seated: A. Williams, K. Maddocks, V. Evans, J.R.G. Stephens
(Captain), G. Thomas, D. Allin, B. Richards.

WALES   NEW ZEALAND

Wales			New Zealand
1. **G. WILLIAMS** London Welsh	FULL-BACKS		1. **R. W. H. SCOTT** Auckland
2. **K. J. JONES** Newport	RIGHT WING	RIGHT WING	4. **A. E. G. ELSOM** Canterbury
3. **G. GRIFFITHS** St. Luke's College & Cardiff	RIGHT CENTRE	CENTRE	5. **J. M. TANNER** Auckland
4. **B. L. WILLIAMS** Cardiff **(Captain)**	LEFT CENTRE	LEFT WING	2. **R. A. JARDEN** Wellington
5. **G. ROWLANDS** Royal Air Force & Cardiff	LEFT WING	SECOND FIVE-EIGHTHS	8. †**B. B. J. FITZPATRICK** Wellington
		FIRST FIVE-EIGHTHS	10. **L. S. HAIG** Otago
6. **C. MORGAN** Cardiff	STAND-OFF		14. **K. DAVIS** or Auckland
7. **W. R. WILLIS** Cardiff	SCRUM-HALF	HALF-BACK	13. **V. D. BEVAN** Wellington
8. **W. O. WILLIAMS** Royal Navy & Swansea	FORWARDS		17. **W. A. McCAW** Southland
9. **D. M. DAVIES** Somerset Police			21. †**W. H. CLARK** Wellington
10. **C. MEREDITH** Neath			16. **R. C. STUART** or Canterbury **(Captain)**
11. **J. R. G. STEPHENS** Neath	KICK-OFF 2.30 P.M. † A new cap		18. †**D. O. OLIVER** Otago
12. **E. R. JOHN** Neath			22. †**G. N. DALZELL** Canterbury
13. †**N. G. DAVIES** London Welsh	Referee : **DR. P. F. COOPER** (Rugby Union)		23. **R. A. WHITE** Poverty Bay
14. **J. A. GWILLIAM** Gloucester	Touch Judges : **IVOR JONES** (Welsh Rugby Union)		28. †**I. J. CLARKE** Waikato
15. **R. C. C. THOMAS** Swansea	**J. T. FITZGERALD** (New Zealand)		29. †**R. C. HEMI** Waikato
			27. **K. L. SKINNER** Otago

Three Neath men were in the pack when Wales last defeated New Zealand at Cardiff Arms Park on 13 December 1953. The score was 13–8.

A packed Gnoll awaits another Neath line-up from 1952/53.

NEW ZEALAND
V

NEATH
and

ABERAVON
(COMBINED)
Chairman of Joint Match Committee
Mr. MELVILLE H. JOHNS

GNOLL GROUND, NEATH
SATURDAY, 23rd JANUARY, 1954

Kick off 2.30 p.m.

SIXPENCE

Programme from the Neath & Aberavon *v*. New
Zealand game played on 23 January 1954 at
The Gnoll.

Trailing 0-11 with fifteen minutes remaining, the combined XV scored the best try of the game when Roy John burst away from his own 25, slipped the ball to Brian Sparks who ran forty yards before handing on to Glyn John who found Courtenay Meredith up in support to score.

Neath RFC 1953/54, a memorable year for Neath as the first clubhouse was opened and the Blacks had a record five players in the Welsh XV. Altogether, nine of this group played for Wales. From left to right, back row: P. Steer, E. Davies, B. Sutcliffe, S.F. Simmons, J. Shufflebotham, C.F. Michael, S. Davies, C. Challinor, G. Moore, W.G. Harrington (all Committee). Standing: A.R. Jones (Committee), H.M. Powell (Committee), W. Millett (Committee), R. Jenkins, D.T. Meredith, E.R. John, D. Thomas, R. Waldron, B. Phillips, G. Jones (Trainer), R. Parker (Baggage man). Seated: K. Maddocks, T. Davies (Treasurer), B. Sparkes, M. John (Chairman), J.R.G. Stephens (Captain), D.M. Evans-Bevan (President), V. Evans, W.A. Griffiths (Secretary), C. Roberts, G. Thomas. Front: D. Allin, B. Richards. Inset: C.C. Meredith.

Neath's five internationals, all capped in 1953/54 were
(from left) Courtenay Meredith, Roy John, Viv Evans,
Rees Stephens, Brian Sparks.

When Wales played Ireland at Lansdowne Road in 1954, four Neath players took the field and a
fifth (Denzil Thomas) had only just left to join Llanelly. From left to right, standing: I. Jones
(Touch Judge), A. Thomas, G. Griffiths, L. Jenkins, R.H. Williams, C.C. Meredith (Neath),
B.V. Meredith, A.W.C. Austin (Referee). Seated: B. Sparkes (Neath), R.C.C. Thomas,
W.R. Willis, J.R.G. Stephens (Neath, Captain), K. Jones, W.O. Williams, V. Evans (Neath).
Front: C.I. Morgan, D. Thomas.

An aerial view of The Gnoll taken in the summer of 1954. The first clubhouse with its gleaming white roof can be seen at the top left (Llantwit) end of the ground and the original stand is next to it. The other three sides of the ground are surrounded by terraces with 'inside the ropes' seating. The field in the bottom left of the picture is the old Bird-in-Hand Field, Neath RFC's home for a brief period in the 1890s.

Neath on the attack against Swansea at St Helen's. Keith Maddocks rounds his opposite number in Neath's 16-5 win on 30 October 1954.

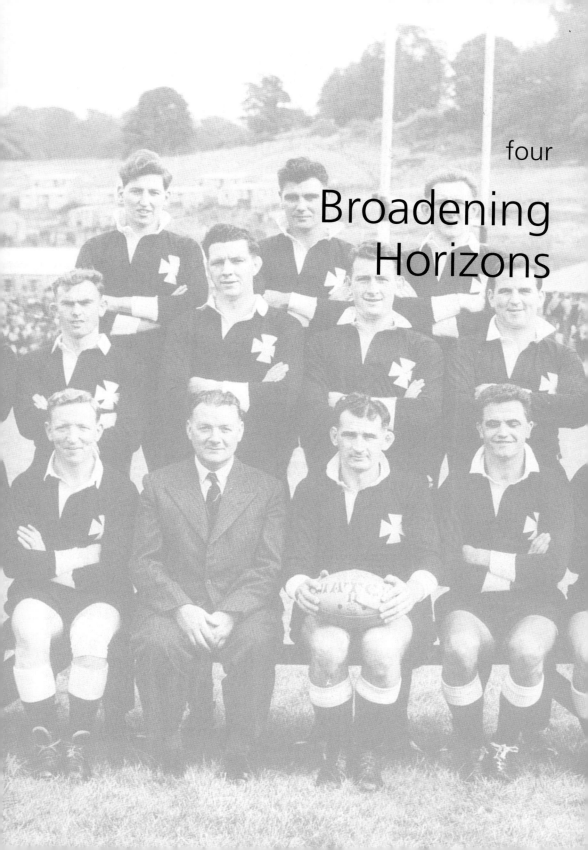

four

Broadening Horizons

Neath has produced a long line of outstanding prop forwards, fourteen of whom have been capped by Wales since the Second World War. Prime among them is surely C.C. (Courtenay) Meredith who won 14 caps and toured with the British Lions to South Africa in 1955 where he commanded total respect from the world's most famous scrummaging nation. Courtenay Meredith was a fearsome scrummager and often opponents would shift positions during a game to get away from him. He was employed in the steelworks at Port Talbot where he rose to become manager of the hot–strip mill.

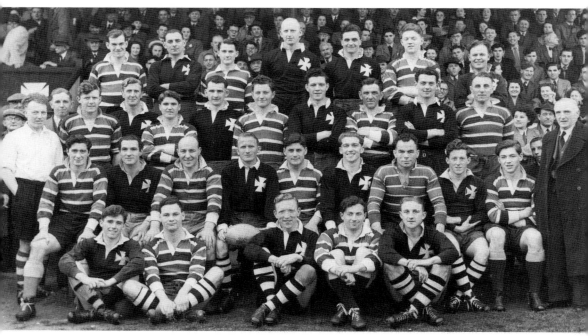

The Gnoll attracted many of the Five Nations championship's finest players during the 1940s and 1950s. The reason? A series of seven games played between Neath and the Rees Stephens' International XV to raise funds for the local YMCA from which Neath Colts and Neath Athletic RFC originally operated. The games were usually spectacular affairs and Neath fared as follows: 1948/49: lost 13-18, 1950/51: won 16-13, 1951/52: lost 24-26, 1952/53: lost 29-31, 1953/54: lost 22-29, 1955/56: lost 26-37, 1956/57: won 9-8. Above are the teams that lined up in the first of those games in 1949. From left to right, back row: A.W. Black, R. Ley, T.J. Brewer, A. Jones, K. Maddocks, A.H. John, E. Rees. Standing: I. David (Referee), T. Mills (Organiser), J.G. Abercrombie, H.O. Edwards, G. Davies, D.T. Meredith, W.B. Holmes, E.R. John, O. Williams, J.R.G. Stephens, J.A. Gwilliam, B. Sutcliffe. Seated: J. Phillips, A. Sullivan, L. Manfield, M. Thomas (Captain), L.B. Cannell, T.J. Griffiths, T.W. Price, F. Williams, R.C.C. Thomas. Front: L. Morgan, W.D. Smith, V. Evans, D.W. Swarbrick, B.L. Jones.

Keith Maddocks scored 17 tries in 1954/55 when scrum-half Gareth Thomas captained Neath. Maddocks was capped once for Wales in their 3–0 win over England in 1956. His regular wing partner on the opposite flank was Cyril Roberts, who bagged 20 tries that season when the Blacks won 22, drew 9 and lost 13 of the 42 games played. They scored 401 points with 280 against and held champions Cardiff to an 11–11 draw.

Above: The 1955 British Lions tour party. The selectors controversially decided that no player over the age of thirty should tour so Rees Stephens, still an outstanding forward for Wales, was omitted. Neath prop Courtenay Meredith could not be overlooked though and, together with Swansea's W.O. Williams and Newport's Bryn Meredith, he set about taming the feared Springbok front row.

Left: Courtenay Meredith hands the ball to scrum-half R.E.G. Jeeps for the Lions in the Third Test at Pretoria on 3 September 1955.

Neath drew 11-11 with French tourists Auvergne on 10 September, 1955. The Auvergne side contained five internationals in full–back Rouan, winger Jean Colombier and forwards Vigier, Chevalier and Domenech. Highlights of the 1955/56 season included beating champions Newport 3-0 and the Irish tour where Neath drew 0-0 with Bective Rangers and beat Old Belvedere 16-8. From left to right, back row: D. Thomas, B. Phillips, B. Sparks. Standing: G. Thomas (Touch Judge), C. Roberts, R. Jenkins, E.R. John, J. Samuel, D. Devereux, D. Allin, H. Davies. Front row: G. Morgan, V. Evans, A.R. Jones (Chairman), D.T. Meredith (Captain), K. Maddocks, G. Hopkins.

Neath RFC 1956/57, skippered by D.T. (Dai) Meredith. Their record was: Played 40, Won 25, Drew 3, Lost 12. Keith Maddocks, who claimed 27 tries that season, set a club record when he scored 6 tries against Ebbw Vale, but the Gwent side were severely depleted as they had double-booked the fixture. In February, full-back Bill Young also bagged 18 points against Newbridge through 6 conversions, a penalty and a dropped goal. From left to right, standing: G. Jones (Trainer), D. Thomas, D. Devereux, J. Samuel, E.R. John, J.R.G. Stephens, B. Phillips, D. Allin, R. Parker (Baggage man). Seated: C.D. Williams, H.A. Davies, C.C. Meredith, A.R. Jones (Chairman), D.T. Meredith (Captain), K. Maddocks, C. Roberts, V. Evans. Front: P. Davies, M. Rogers, W. Young, J. Weaver.

The final match in the series against Rees Stephens' International XV took place on Thursday 26 September 1957 when players from all the Five Nations teams graced The Gnoll. From left to right, back row: D. Davies, S. Quinlan, E. Thomas, M. Chevalier, T. Palmer, A. Richards, R. Waldron. Standing: P. Steer, T. Davies, W. Harvey, B. Meredith, T. Thomas, E. Michie, E. Walters, G. Davies, E.R. John, H. Nicholls, J. Samuel, J. Bouquet, W. Young, D. Gardner (YMCA Secretary), D.T. Meredith. Seated: G. Hastings, A. Stephens, W.O. Williams, D.B. Rees (Captain), R.C.C. Thomas (Captain), A. Prosser-Harries, E. Davies, A. O'Connor, R. Jenkins, A.A. Mulligan, W. Millett (Chairman). Front: J. Weaver, B. Richards, V. Evans.

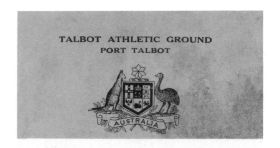

TALBOT ATHLETIC GROUND
PORT TALBOT

AUSTRALIA

v.

NEATH and ABERAVON

OFFICIAL
PROGRAMME
6d.

Saturday, 28th December, 1957
KICK-OFF 2.15 P.M.

Left and below: Neath & Aberavon came closest to beating a touring team when they were pipped 3-5 by the Australians at Aberavon on 28 December 1957. John Thornett (who would later return as captain of the 1966/67 Wallabies) scored the visitors' try, Harvey converting. There were two changes to the side published in the programme, Neath's Don Crowley taking the place of John Collins and scoring the home side's try, and Aberavon prop Len Cunningham taking over from Don Devereux. The two replaced players would earn their first caps when Wales defeated Australia the following week.

AUSTRALIA			NEATH & ABERAVON	
	FULL BACKS			
1. T. G. CURLEY N.S.W.			1. W. YOUNG NEATH	
	THREE-QUARTERS			
7. G. BAILEY N.S.W.	RIGHT WING	LEFT WING	2. J. COLLINS ABERAVON	*D. Crowley*
2. J. K. LENEHAN N.S.W.	OUTSIDE CENTRE	LEFT CENTRE	3. W. PASCOE ABERAVON	
8. J. M. POTTS N.S.W.	INSIDE CENTRE	RIGHT CENTRE	4. T. THOMAS NEATH	
6. R. PHELPS N.S.W.	LEFT WING	RIGHT WING	5. C. ROBERTS NEATH	
	HALF-BACKS			
11. R. M. HARVEY N.S.W.	FIVE-EIGHTH	OUTSIDE HALF	6. C. ASHTON ABERAVON	
13. D. M. CONNOR QUEENSLAND	INSIDE HALF	INSIDE HALF	7. T. O'CONNOR (Capt.) ABERAVON	
	FORWARDS			
25. R. A. DAVIDSON (Capt.) (N.S.W.)			8. C. MEREDITH NEATH	
29. J. V. BROWN N.S.W.			9. R. JENKINS NEATH	
24. N. SHEHADIE N.S.W.		*L. cunningham*	10. D. DEVERAUX NEATH	
23. A. R. MILLER N.S.W.			11. J. BAMSEY ABERAVON	
22. D. M. EMANUEL N.S.W.			12. J. SAMUEL NEATH	
15. P. FENWICKE N.S.W.			13. R. O'CONNOR ABERAVON	
17. N. M. HUGHES N.S.W.	Referee: Mr. A. WILLIAMS, (Newport)		14. I. PROSSER ABERAVON	
19. J. THORNETT N.S.W.	Touch-Judge: G. N. VAUGHAN	Touch-Judge: G. P. STEER (Neath)	15. P. JONES ABERAVON	

Message from Mr. Glyn Stephens, J.P.

(President of the Welsh Rugby Union)

TODAY'S special match in aid of the British Empire and Commonwealth Games of 1958, should provide a fitting end to the 1956-57 Rugby season. When the idea was first mooted, the Welsh Rugby Union gave the matter full and serious consideration before deciding unanimously to seek the aid of the other Home Countries.

The very fact that the strongest side that could be chosen from the other Home Countries will take the field to oppose Wales in today's match, is full proof of the willingness of England, Scotland and Ireland to help make the Games a success.

The Welsh Rugby Union has worked in close co-operation with the Cardiff Rugby Club, to whom a big debt of gratitude is owed, to ensure the successful staging of this match and I look forward to a game of Rugby worthy of the occasion. The Empire Games have done a great deal of good for amateur sport and side by side with Rugby football it has helped develop a healthy love and appreciation of sport among the young men and women of the Commonwealth.

Rugby Football is spreading its wings throughout the world and now after long and friendly relationships with New Zealand, Australia and South Africa, we turn westwards to Canada, and this month a powerful team representing the Barbarians will visit that great Commonwealth country. Nine of the Barbarians are in action today.

Welshmen like to think that they have contributed to the development of the Game and are proud of their happy record and cordial relationships with other Countries.

As President of the Welsh Rugby Union, I welcome players, officials and spectators to the Cardiff Arms Park today. I hope you will enjoy a happy afternoon's football and prepare the way for a successful Games on the same ground next year.

I am confident that Wales will give the athletes of the Commonwealth the welcome they deserve, and I know that the Cardiff Arms Park will give them a welcome worthy of true sportsmen. On with the Game !

Right: Glyn Stephens was president of the WRU in 1956/57. He and Rees were the first father and son pairing to captain Wales and then the first father and son to sit on the WRU committee. This is Glyn's presidential programme address for the special Welsh XV *v.* An International XV, played at Cardiff Arms Park on Saturday 6 April 1957, a game played to raise funds for the Commonwealth Games.

Below: Glyn's son Rees captained Wales that day in his final appearance in a Welsh shirt.

A WELSH XV				AN INTERNATIONAL XV	
1.	**T. E. DAVIES** Llanelly	FULL BACKS		1.	**P. J. BERKERY** (Lansdowne and Ireland)
		THREE-QUARTERS			
2.	**G. HOWELLS** Llanelly	RIGHT WING	LEFT WING	5.	**A. J. O'REILLY** (Old Belvedere and Ireland)
3.	**C. DAVIES** Llanelly	RIGHT CENTRE	LEFT CENTRE	4.	**J. BUTTERFIELD** (Northampton and England)
4.	**G. WELLS** Cardiff	LEFT CENTRE	RIGHT CENTRE	3.	**W. P. C. DAVIES** (Harlequins and England)
5.	**R. WILLIAMS** Llanelly	LEFT WING	RIGHT WING	2.	**A. R. SMITH** (Cambridge University and Scotland)
		HALF BACKS			
6.	**C. I. MORGAN** Cardiff	STAND-OFF		6.	**R. M. BARTLETT** (Harlequins and England)
7.	**L. WILLIAMS** Cardiff	SCRUM		7.	**R. E. G. JEEPS** (Northampton and England)
		FORWARDS			
8.	**H. MORGAN** Llanelly			8.	**T. ELLIOT** (Gala and Scotland)
9.	**B. V. MEREDITH** London Welsh			9.	**E. EVANS** (Sale and England) (**CAPTAIN**)
10.	**R. PROSSER** Pontypool			10.	**B. G. WOOD** (Garryowen and Ireland)
11.	**J. R. G. STEPHENS** Neath (**CAPTAIN**)			11.	**R. W. D. MARQUES** (Cambridge University and England)
12.	**R. H. WILLIAMS** Llanelly			12.	**T. E. REID** (London Irish and Ireland)
13.	**R. J. ROBINS** Pontypridd	Referee: **Dr. P. F. COOPER** (R.F.U.)		13.	**A. R. HIGGINS** (Liverpool and England)
14.	**J. FAULL** Swansea			14.	**J. T. GREENWOOD** (Perthshire Academicals and Scotland)
15.	**R. H. DAVIES** London Welsh and Oxford University	KICK-OFF 3.30 P.M.		15.	**P. G. D. ROBBINS** (Oxford University and England)

Touch Judge: **Mr. L. GRIFFIN** (Blaina) — Touch Judge: **Mr. E. SELBY** (Briton Ferry)

Above: Neath RFC 1957/58, skippered by Courtenay Meredith, won 23 drew 4 and lost 19 of their 46 games. They scored 385 points with 277 against. Centre Terry Thomas scored 12 tries and they drew 3-3 with champions Cardiff. From left to right, back row: D. Crowley, D. Newton, R. Jenkins, T. Thomas, R. Parker. Standing: R. Waldron, E. Thomas, J. Samuel, J.R.G. Stephens, D. Roberts, L. Harris, G. Evans, M. Morgan, G. Jones (Trainer). Seated: L. Morgan (Treasurer), C. Roberts, E.R. John, C.C. Meredith (Captain), W. Millett (Chairman), W.A. Griffiths (Secretary). Front row: J. Evans, J. Weaver, J.C. Hopkins, J. Edwards.

Prop Ron Waldron captained Neath in 1959/60. Steelworker Waldron made his debut for Neath from Neath Colts against Rosslyn Park on 13 September 1952 and soon earned a regular spot as 'the young apprentice in a pack of master craftsmen'. He played for Devonport Services and the Barbarians and was chosen for Wales against Ireland in 1962 only for the game to be held over until the following season due to a smallpox epidemic. He was then omitted from the replay, toured South Africa without winning a cap in 1964, and must have all but given up hope of ever winning a cap. But perseverance eventually paid off and he at last took his place in the Welsh XV that won the Triple Crown in 1965. He retired in 1968, was elected onto the Neath committee and became coach until 1974/75. After a spell coaching Neath Colts, Neath & District Youth and Welsh Youth, he returned to his beloved Gnoll once more and helped guide the Blacks to their greatest days before becoming national coach.

Right: Perhaps Neath's blackest day occurred on 9 January 1960 when young lock (No. 8) forward Alun Davies, a twenty-three-year-old colliery fitter from Pontrhydyfen, broke his neck in a freak accident in Neath's 8-3 win over Pontypool. The initial newspaper report does not portray the seriousness of his injury and tragically Davies was paralysed, never to recover.

Opposite below: Neath RFC 1958/59, led by scrum-half D.B. Rees. The Blacks played 40, won 21, drew 6 and lost 13, with 317 points for and 235 against. Cyril Roberts scored 18 tries and Terry Thomas got 62 points. From left to right, back row: G. Jones (Trainer), D. Richards, D. Crowley, M. Morgan, A. Lewis, R. Parker (Baggage man). Standing: A. Davies, D.S. Hill, B. Thomas, J.R.G. Stephens, J. Dodd, R. Waldron, H. Harries. Seated: C. Roberts, M. Williams, S. Davies (Chairman), D.B. Rees (Captain), J. Hopkins, T. Thomas.

Triumph and tragedy in Neath match

(By JEFF HOCKEY)
Neath 8pts.; Pontypool 3pts.

THE brilliant fighting spirit of 14 Neath men earned them their deserved victory over Pontypool, on Saturday, in the best match seen at the Gnoll this season. In addition, they must have embarrassed the Welsh selectors—to say the least—who have thought no Neath men good enough to play against England to-morrow (Saturday).

It was a game of triumph and tragedy. The tragedy came near the end of the first half, when Neath's 23-year-old lock forward Alun Davies left the field with an injury to his neck and back.

Alun had to be carried off on a stretcher and was immediately rushed into hospital, in a serious condition.

The triumph came for the whole team, who have at last returned to that long lost form and looked even the better side of the two with only fourteen men.

The match was also a personal triumph for both Terry Thomas and Cyril Roberts. Thomas, the most dangerous player on the field, burst through the visitors' defence time and time again.

His brilliant running and kicking must have made the Welsh selectors wish they could change their minds about ignoring him from the international team.

Cyril Roberts was the All Blacks hero of the day, scoring his side's two tries in really grand style.

The first came from a pass from Terry Thomas, after the centre had done most of the spade work. But Roberts collected beautifully, outstripped a couple of defenders and touched down near the posts. Graham Hodgson converted.

SPECTACULAR

His second try was even more spectacular than the first. The winger seized on a mix up between Pontypool winger David Evans and centre Graham Tovey, raced along the touch from just inside his own half, and neatly swerved past the full-back.

But Pontypool sadly missed their stars. Welsh internationals Ray Prosser and Malcolm Price

were both out of the side, as was, of course, newly capped scrum-half Colin Evans.

With their depleted side and Neath's remarkable return to form, Pontypool never looked the masters. They had more of the play in the second half, but could not break through the cast iron All Blacks defence.

ON FORM

Neath's other trialist full-back, Graham Hodgson, was also on form. Whilst most of the players were suffering from numbed hands because of the bitterly cold wind, Hodgson caught, kicked and positioned himself perfectly throughout.

His cool head and quick thinking pushed the Pontypool team back off the Neath line several times.

Billy Bevan, of Seven Sisters, deputising for Don Crowley in the centre, and winger Arnold Williams both had good games and both tackled really well.

Crymant outside-half Rhys Thomas, a last minute substitute for Doug. Allin, hit it off perfectly with scrum-half Dai Rees and between them formed a dangerous half-back combination.

Thomas, with wing-forwards Dai Morgan and Eifion Thomas managed to completely bottle up Pontypool's dangerous fly-half, Benny Jones, and also subdued the visiting backs.

In the pack, Cambridge University student Brian Thomas played brilliantly. His work in the line-out was excellent and he was always dangerous in the loose.

FINE WORK

He was partnered by Bryn, coch's second row forward Dai Davies. Davies is another good boy and did some fine loose work. He also showed he had a good kick with one or two long range touch-finders.

John Dodds and Meirion Bell were very useful in the depleted pack and Dodds was especially good in rallying the pack near the end.

Neath's hooker and find of the season Herbie Murphy, of Glais, got far more of the ball in the tight than his opponent Haydn Pugh.

But Pugh's great work in the loose was rewarded with his side's only try mid-way through the second half. This came from a loose maul near the Neath line and Pugh ploughed his way over.

There is no doubt that if Saturday's big England-Wales clash provides half the open rugby and thrills of this game, it will be well worth watching.

There was a poor crowd at the game, but if Neath continue to play this rugby then that is the sort of stuff to have the enthusiasts flocking back in large numbers.

Neath Rugby Football Ground

SPECIAL

BENEFIT MATCH

MONDAY, 2nd MAY, 1960

KICK-OFF 6.30 p.m.

Aberavon & Neath (Combined)

VERSUS

Llanelly & Swansea (Combined)

ALUN DAVIES

☆ *The entire proceeds of sale of Match Tickets and Programmes will be devoted to the Alun Davies Benefit Fund*

THE ORGANISING COMMITTEE WISH TO THANK THE "SOUTH WALES EVENING POST," WHO VERY KINDLY VOLUNTEERED TO DEFRAY THE COST OF THESE PROGRAMMES.

Ladies and Gentlemen,

On behalf of the Neath Rugby Football Club I would like to take this opportunity of expressing our sincere thanks to all those who have so readily responded to our appeal on behalf of the Alun Davies Benefit Fund. Contributions and donations have been received from so many individuals, Rugby Clubs, Social Clubs, Hotels, Works Committees and various Organisations that it is not possible to thank you individually, therefore I will do so collectively.

The major contribution to the Fund is, of course, the proceeds of the sale of tickets for to-day's match, and for making this possible I say to our Aberavon, Llanelly and Swansea friends, "THANK YOU" for so generously offering your help and co-operation. Also to Mr. Gwynne Walters for taking charge of the match! and last, but by no means least, the Welsh Rugby Union for extending the playing season to enable the match to take place to-day. This concession is much appreciated.

Now about Alun himself. Our latest news is that there is a slight improvement in his condition, which is revealed in his cheerful countenance. It is understood that respiration is easier, and discomfort is not so severe. Alun's courage and fortitude have earned many tributes from those who administer treatment, and are regarded as noble and worthy contributions to the efforts to effect a cure.

It is pleasing to learn that members of Alun's family intend to be present at this match. A special welcome is accorded to his brother Gareth, who has resided at Oxford since Alun's transfer to that city.

I know you will join with me in conveying to Alun our best wishes for a full and quick recovery.

Thank you.

W. G. HARRINGTON,

Chairman, Neath R.F.C.

Printed by the Guardian Press (Neath) Ltd., and published by the Neath Rugby Supporters' Club. Hon. Secretary : Ron Davies, "Littledene," 54 Lewis Road, Neath. Telephone No. Neath 269.

Aberavon—Neath (Combined)   44

Colours—ALL BLACK

Llanelly—Swansea (Combined)   29

Colours—RED JERSEY, WHITE SHORTS

Aberavon—Neath		Position	Llanelly—Swansea		
1—GRAHAM HODGSON	(N)	FULL BACK	TERRY DAVIES	(L)°	1
2—JOHN COLLINS	(A)°	RIGHT WING	RAY WILLIAMS *LEMON*	(L)°	2
3—DAVE THOMAS	(A)	RIGHT CENTRE	~~BRIAN DAVIES~~	(L)	3
4—ALAN THOMAS	(N)	LEFT CENTRE	C. RODERICK	(S)	4
5—KEN THOMAS	(A)	LEFT WING	~~DEN DEBB~~ *R HARDING*	(S)°	5
6—~~CLIFF ASHTON~~ *E. THOMAS*	(A)°	OUTSIDE HALF	BRYAN RICHARDS	(S)°	6
7—D. B. REES *Zca*	(N)	INSIDE HALF	D. O. BRACE (Capt.)	(L)°	7
8—LEN CUNNINGHAM	(A)°	FORWARDS	~~HOWARD DAVIES~~	(L)	8
9—RHYS LOVELUCK	(A)	,,	N. GALE	(S)°	9
10—RON WALDRON (Capt.)	(N)	,,	GWYN LEWIS	(S)	10
11—JOHN DODDS	(N)	,,	R. H. WILLIAMS	(L)°	11
12—D. DAVIES	(N)	,,	~~W. O. WILLIAMS~~ *ROWLANDS*	(S)°	12
13—PETER JONES	(A)	,,	MARLSTON MORGAN	(L)	13
14—JOHN DAVIES	(N)	,,	GORDON MORRIS	(S)	14
15—RORY O'CONNOR	(A)°	,,	~~JOHN LELEU~~ *W. JENKINS*	(S)°	15

Referee : GWYNNE WALTERS (Gowerton)

° Indicates International.

The Neath team and the rugby fraternity rallied round to help Alun Davies. Various events were organised, including this benefit match played on Monday 2 May 1960 when Neath & Aberavon combined to take on Llanelly & Swansea. The teams were skippered by Ron Waldron and Onllwyn Bruce respectively.

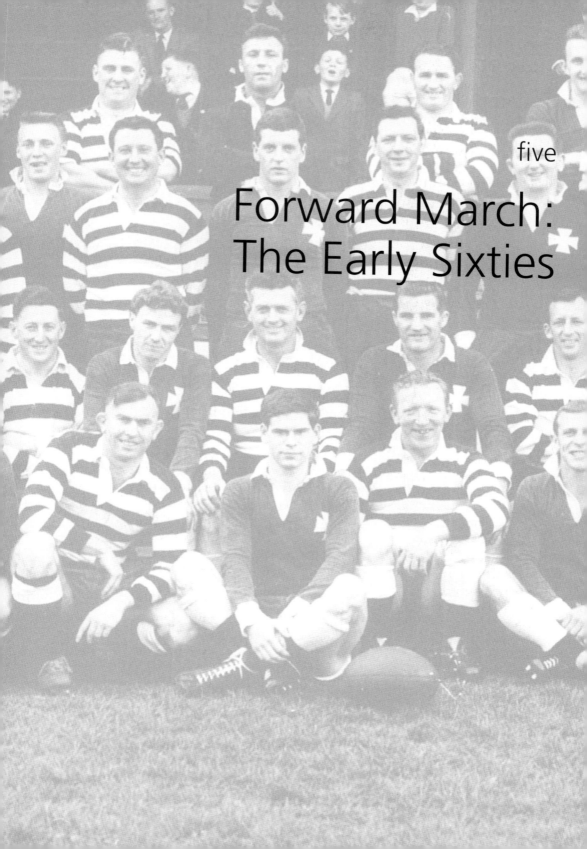

five

Forward March:
The Early Sixties

Neath visited Dublin in November 1961 when they drew 6-6 with Bective Rangers and beat Old Belvedere 16-0. The Neath party included the following: from left to right, back row: D. Davies, Arnold Williams, R. Williams (Committee), -?-, -?-, P. Davies. Standing: E. Jones, S. Davies, Trevor Thomas, A. Butler, J. Davies, G. Ball, J. Roberts, R. Waldron, G. Jones, T. Dargavel, R. Parker, -?-, -?-, J.R.G. Stephens. Seated: R. Thomas, H.M. Powell, M. Williams (Captain), -?-, A. Dix. Front: L. Davies, R. Richards, G.T.R. Hodgson, G. Davies.

The programme from the Neath v. Aberavon match, 5 April 1962. Aberavon were probably at the peak of their powers at the time with six Welsh internationals and a future England cap in second-row David Watt (Bristol) but Neath beat them 3-0. Neath, unusually, had no capped men in their team although Grahame Hodgson, Ron Evans (later Bridgend and South Wales Police), Ron Waldron and John Davies would later represent their country.

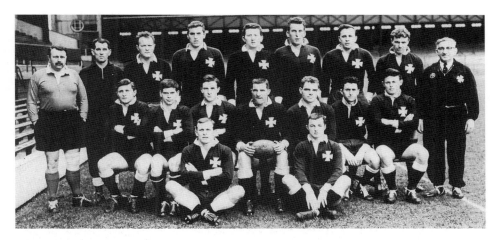

Neath paid their only visit to Twickenham to play Harlequins on 7 April 1962. The match resulted in a scoreless draw. Young Neath Athletic outside half Ceri Hopkins (whose career was curtailed by a serious knee injury) recalls that the wind swirled around Twickenham and helped him put in some fifty-yard touch-finders that touch-judge Cyril Niven might have exaggerated. The Blacks have only played Harlequins once since, in the European Cup of 1996/97, when the Harlequins included Neath brothers Glyn and Gareth Llewellyn. From left to right, standing: -?- (Referee), C. Niven (Touch Judge), R. Waldron, B. Thomas, D. Davies, P. Davies, F. Mitchell, A. Dix, G. Jones (Trainer). Seated: R. Thomas, G. Ball, D. Richards, J. Dodd (Captain), M. Williams, R. Richards, C. Hopkins. Front: G.T.R. Hodgson, K. Evans.

At the end of the 1961/62 season, which they finished with an impressive record (Played 46, Won 32, Drew 5, Lost 9, Points For 522, Points Against 222), Neath played a Past XV on 27 April 1962. From left to right, back row: Dudley Thomas, Ernie Jones, G. Lewis, A. Butler. Standing: I. David (Referee), C. Niven (Touch Judge), F. Mitchell, H. Harries, J. Bailey, G. Evans, J. Davies, E.R. John, D. Davies, W. Brennan, E. Davies, S. Davies (Touch Judge). Seated: J.C. Hopkins, R. Evans, F. Williams, A. Dix, J.R.G. Stephens (Past Captain), J. Dodd (Present Captain), D.B. Rees, R. Thomas, M. Thomas. Front: H. Watkins, C. Hopkins, R. Jenkins, G. Ball, V. Evans, G.T.R. Hodgson, Elwyn Jones, D. Richards.

Near right: Hooker Morlais Williams captained Neath in 1962/63. Reared in nearby Seven Sisters, the steely haired Williams was one of the most adept strikers around and his likeable nature, like those of his props Dodd and Waldron, belied a gritty determination on the field. The Neath front row of the 1960s never took a step back and it was only the consistency of Llanelli's Norman Gale that kept Morlais out of the Welsh team. The trio was selected en bloc for the Welsh

trial in 1965 and easily took the head count but only Waldron ever won Welsh honours. John Dodd, Neath RFC captain for three seasons, 1960/61, 1961/62 and 1963/64, was a product of Porthcawl and played briefly for Cardiff before joining Neath. He later served on the Neath committee.

Right: 28 September 1962 was an auspicious occasion for Neath as they played, and beat, Glamorgan County 15-6 in a match to mark the opening of the new stand.

Little to cheer in celebration match

Neath 15pts.; Glamorgan 6pts.

THERE was little to cheer in this celebration match, arranged to follow the official opening of the new grandstand at the Gnoll. Neath won the match comfortably enough, but the play was never inspiring or as carefree as it should have been for such an occasion, **writes Elfed Bowen.**

Neath owed their success to their pack, who played with far more zest than they did against Aberavon on Saturday.

Welsh selector Cliff Jones was present and he must have noted the fine performances of at least two of the Neath players. Full-back Grahame Hodgson had another outstanding game and kicked the conversions of the three Neath tries. Another player who should have caught the selector's eye was second-row forward Brian Thomas. He jumped brilliantly in the lines-out, while also playing a full role in all other departments of play.

The Glamorgan three-quarters appeared faster than their opposite numbers and were far more eager to play entertaining football. There were times when they combined well only to lose scoring chances by last-second errors. Their right-wing, Steve Hughes, of Cardiff, was particularly prone to this failing. He several times broke clear with skilful running only to make a wrong decision with the Neath line waiting to be crossed.

The three Neath tries were scored by the forwards, who worked with greater cohesion, drive and enthusiasm in this game.

Prop-forward Ron Waldron, who was always prominent in the Neath pack, scored the first when he crossed in the corner after eight minutes' play.

Just before half-time Glamorgan reduced the lead when Graham Gittings, the Pontypridd prop-forward, landed a 30-yard penalty goal.

When a scrum was called near the Glamorgan line, the Neath supporters gave their customary instruction to the pack to "P-U-S-H." The forwards obliged and sent the pack reeling for Dai Davies to be credited with a push-over try.

Waldron made the opening for Neath's third try when he broke away from a line-out on the Glamorgan 25 before passing to lock-forward John Davies, who crossed for the touch-down.

Glamorgan's try followed a good break from their skipper, Alan Price, Maesteg.

He ran strongly before sending a well-timed pass to Billy Griffiths, Pontypridd, who handed to Mike Thomas, the Swansea wing-forward, who crossed for an unconverted try.

Neath won the Snelling Sevens in 1963/64.
From left to right, standing: H. Rees,
W.D. Morris, Peter Davies. Seated: K. Evans,
M. Williams (Captain), M. Davies,
R. Thomas.

Right: Aberavon and Neath
combined to take on Wilson
Whineray's All Blacks on
2 November 1963.

Opposite below: Neath RFC,
1962/63. From left to right, back
row: K. Bell, F. Mitchell, R. Davies,
E. Davies, A. Dix, S. Davies (Touch
Judge). Middle row: G. Jones
(Trainer), D. Davies, B. Thomas,
P. Davies, A. Butler, W.D. Morris,
R. Waldron, H. Rees. Seated:
R. Thomas, G.T.R. Hodgson,
H.M. Powell (Chairman),
M. Williams (Captain), J. Dodd,
G.Ball. Front: L. Tregonning,
K. Evans, M. Davies, -?- (Ballboy).

TALBOT ATHLETIC GROUND
PORT TALBOT

NEW ZEALAND
v.
ABERAVON & NEATH

OFFICIAL
PROGRAMME
6d.

SATURDAY, 2nd NOVEMBER, 1963
Kick-off 2.45 p.m.

NEW ZEALAND   ABERAVON & NEATH

		FULL BACKS		
1	**D. B. CLARKE** WAIKATO			*G. HODGSON** 15 NEATH

		THREE-QUARTERS		
3	**M. J. DICK** AUCKLAND	RIGHT WING	LEFT WING	**R. STADDON** 14 ABERAVON
5	**P. F. LITTLE** AUCKLAND	RIGHT CENTRE	LEFT CENTRE	**B. JONES** 13 ABERAVON
12	**D. A. ARNOLD** CANTERBURY	LEFT CENTRE	RIGHT CENTRE	*D. THOMAS** 12 ABERAVON
4	**I. S. T. SMITH** OTAGO	LEFT WING	RIGHT WING	**H. REES** 11 NEATH

		HALF-BACKS		
14	**M. A. HEREWINI** AUCKLAND	OUTSIDE HALF	OUTSIDE HALF	**C. JONES** 10 ABERAVON
11	**K. C. BRISCOE** TARANAKI	INSIDE HALF	INSIDE HALF	*T. O'CONNOR** 9 ABERAVON

		FORWARDS		
21	**K. F. GRAY** WELLINGTON			*P. MORGAN (Capt.)** 1 ABERAVON
15	**D. YOUNG** CANTERBURY			**M. WILLIAMS** 2 NEATH
17	**W. J. WHINERAY (Capt.)** AUCKLAND			*L. CUNNINGHAM** 3 ABERAVON
26	**D. J. GRAHAM** CANTERBURY			*B. THOMAS** 4 NEATH
22	**C. E. MEADS** KING COUNTRY			**D. DAVIES** 5 NEATH
29	**K. A. NELSON** OTAGO			**A. BUTLER** 6 NEATH
23	**S. T. MEADS** KING COUNTRY			**D. MORRIS** 8 NEATH
24	**A. J. STEWART** CANTERBURY			**P. JONES** 7 ABERAVON

Referee :
Mr. F. G. PRICE
(Blaenavon)

Touch-Judge: Touch-Judge:
SID DAVIES (Neath)   P. T. WALSH (N.Z.)

*Internationals

Above: Brian Thomas on his way to scoring his only international try against Scotland in 1964. He is supported by Llanelli's Norman Gale and Newport's Brian Price.

Right: On 8 October, 1964, Neath switched on their floodlights when they drew 8-8 with a strong International XV.

Opposite above: A pre-match thunderstorm made conditions difficult, and the combined XV were heading for a 6-6 draw thanks to a try by Aberavon flanker Peter Jones (whose son Lyn would later play for and coach Neath) and a Hodgson penalty. New Zealand tries came from Smith and Little and they pounced for a late third by prop Ken Gray, which full-back Don Clarke converted.

Opposite below: Neath RFC boasted a ground record in 1963/64 when they won 35, drew 2 and lost just 7 of the 44 games played, scoring 568 points with 181 against. Grahame Hodgson scored 115 points. From left to right, back row: D. Jones, K. Bell, R. Thomas, M. Bishop. Standing: R. Davies, W.D. Morris, D. Davies, B. Thomas, A. Butler, A. Dix, G. Ball. Seated: R. Waldron, J. Dodd (Captain), B. Dennis (Chairman), G.T.R. Hodgson, H. Rees. Front: M. Davies, K. Evans.

MEMORABLE NIGHT FOR NEATH R.F.C.

Neath 8pts.; International XV 8pts.

NEATH had a splendid send-off into the floodlight world when they played against an International XV at the Gnoll last week. Rarely have the "All Blacks" looked or played more impressively **(writes Tony Crocker).**

The game produced open and extremely exciting rugby from start to finish, and thrilled the crowd, for there was little to compare it with the usual type of "exhibition" match.

The Internationals were first to score after nine minutes, with a try from Wrench converted by Terry Davies, but Neath were quick to reply when, three minutes later, Keith Bell raced over the line. Alan Butler converted bringing Neath to level terms. It was outside-half Keith Evans who gave Neath an 8-5 lead at the interval, when he scored a fine opportunist try shortly after.

Evans played well and, as always, he and his partner, Martyn Davies, were a formidable pair at half-back. Martyn used the touch-line to the best advantage and was also the source of most of Neath's attacks.

Playing his best game so far this season, Glen Ball was always a dangerous man when on the move, and the international defence had their work cut out in "marking" him. He and left centre Roy Thomas were prominent in the many sparkling sweeps upfield.

David Watkins the international outside-half, supplied plenty of entertainment with his nippy dart-like all-action rushes. On one occasion he nearly scored, but an excellent tackle from full-back Grahame Hodgson saved Neath.

The battle of the forwards was truly fought and the outstanding Wales No. 8, Alun Pask, played brilliantly, as did his opposite number, Dave Morris. Always to the fore, the Neath front row men, John Dodd, Morlais Williams and Ron Waldron, worked hard and were noticeable in the loose scrummages.

For the internationals, the Italian guests, Serge Lan Franchi and Francesco Zani were hard workers and were ably supported by Gerry Protheroe and Roger Michaelson.

Scores for Neath came from Keith Bell and Keith Evans. Alan Butler converted Bell's try. For the international side, D. F. B. Wrench scored a try, which was converted by Terry Davies. Davies also kicked a penalty in the second half and by so doing equalised.

Neath's £10,000 floodlights were officially switched on by Mr. Martyn Evans-Bevan.

Neath RFC extended their ground record in 1964/65 when they won 38, drew 3 and lost 10 games. Winger Howard Rees scored 24 tries and back-rower Alan Butler got 117 points as Neath piled up 633 scored with only 270 against. From left to right, back row: Doug Jones, K. Bell, J. Dodd, M. Bishop. Standing: R. Davies, W.D. Morris, D. Davies, B. Thomas, A. Butler, A. Dix, H. Rees. Seated: R. Waldron, G.T.R. Hodgson (Captain), B. Dennis (Team Secretary), R. Thomas, G. Ball. Front: K. Evans, M. Davies.

Wales international full-back Grahame Hodgson led Neath in 1964/65. St Luke's College Exeter-product Hodgson joined the All Blacks in 1958/59 and went on to score over 1,500 points for the club. The Bridgend-based schoolmaster was an immaculate example of the full-back's art and was an imperious member of Neath's 1966/67 championship-winning side. Capped 15 times for Wales, he dislocated a shoulder the following season and was player/coach in 1971/72 when Neath won the cup. He later returned as coach in 1976/77 when Neath enjoyed a very productive season.

six

'On, On, On...'

Neath's tradition for producing the best forwards in Wales continued in the 1960s with the emergence of second-row Brian Thomas. A Neath man through and through, Brian first came to prominence as a rugged second row and captain of the unbeaten Neath Grammar School XV, and was soon earning his spurs for the All Blacks. Totally uncompromising in his approach, he won three Blues at Cambridge University before returning to Neath and a position in the Steel Company of Wales. He won the first of his 21 caps for Wales against England in 1963 and scored a try against Scotland in 1964. Unaccountably ignored by the Lions selectors in 1966, he captained Neath to their seventh championship in 1966/67 as the Welsh All Blacks, forward control assured, marched on at scrums and mauls to their captain's clarion call of 'On, On, On!' And on, on, on it was in a relentless advance towards the title. On the field, Brian's last fling, as it were, was in seeing his beloved Neath become the first winners of the WRU Cup in 1971/72, but he returned to The Gnoll a decade later as team manager and masterminded the club's rise to the top in the 1980s and 1990s.

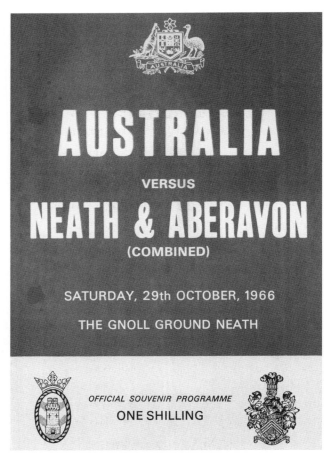

The programme from the 1966/67 tourist game.

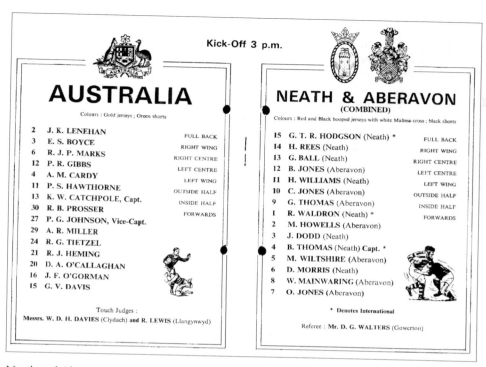

Kick-Off 3 p.m.

AUSTRALIA

Colours : Gold jerseys ; Green shorts

2	J. K. LENEHAN	FULL BACK
3	E. S. BOYCE	RIGHT WING
6	R. J. P. MARKS	RIGHT CENTRE
12	P. R. GIBBS	LEFT CENTRE
4	A. M. CARDY	LEFT WING
11	P. S. HAWTHORNE	OUTSIDE HALF
13	K. W. CATCHPOLE, Capt.	INSIDE HALF
30	R. B. PROSSER	FORWARDS
27	P. G. JOHNSON, Vice-Capt.	
29	A. R. MILLER	
24	R. G. TIETZEL	
21	R. J. HEMING	
20	D. A. O'CALLAGHAN	
16	J. F. O'GORMAN	
15	G. V. DAVIS	

Touch Judges :
Messrs. W. D. H. DAVIES (Clydach) **and R. LEWIS** (Llangynwyd)

NEATH & ABERAVON
(COMBINED)

Colours : Red and Black hooped jerseys with white Maltese cross ; black shorts

15	G. T. R. HODGSON (Neath) *	FULL BACK
14	H. REES (Neath)	RIGHT WING
13	G. BALL (Neath)	RIGHT CENTRE
12	B. JONES (Aberavon)	LEFT CENTRE
11	H. WILLIAMS (Neath)	LEFT WING
10	C. JONES (Aberavon)	OUTSIDE HALF
9	G. THOMAS (Aberavon)	INSIDE HALF
1	R. WALDRON (Neath) *	FORWARDS
2	M. HOWELLS (Aberavon)	
3	J. DODD (Neath)	
4	B. THOMAS (Neath) Capt. *	
5	M. WILTSHIRE (Aberavon)	
6	D. MORRIS (Neath)	
8	W. MAINWARING (Aberavon)	
7	O. JONES (Aberavon)	

* Denotes International

Referee : **Mr. D. G. WALTERS** (Gowerton)

Neath and Aberavon combined once more to play the Australians, but lost 3-9 at The Gnoll.

NEATH v. ABERAVON

SATURDAY, FEBRUARY 18th, 1967. Kick-off 3.30 p.m.

NEATH		ABERAVON
15 **Graham Hodgson**	*Full Back*	Paul Wheeler 15
14 **Howard Rees**	*Right Wing*	Brian Flynn 14
13 **Glen Ball** ...	*Right Centre*	Cyril Jones 13
12 **Brian Davies**	*Left Centre*	David Thomas 12
11 **Hywel Williams**	*Left Wing*	Keith Bell 11
10 **Keith Evans**	*Outside Half*	Bernard Locke 10
9 **Martyn Davies**	*Inside Half*	Gareth Thomas 9
1 **Ron Waldron**		Phil Morgan 1
2 **Morlais Williams**		Morton Howells 2
3 **Walter Williams**		Eric Jones 3
4 **Brian Thomas** (Captain)	*Forwards*	Max Wiltshire 4 (Captain)
5 **Jeff Pyles**		Billy Mainwaring 5
6 **Randall Davies**		John Davies 6
8 **Dave Morris**		Bob Wanbon 8
7 **Meirion Prosser**		Omri Jones 7

Referee : Mr. I. T. George, Beaufort

Neath led the Welsh championship from the start of the 1966/67 season and did not lose a game until December, when they lost 6-9 at Cardiff. Their charge to the championship included this game at Aberavon on Saturday 18 February 1967 with Mr Ivor George (later Ebbw Vale's hon. secretary) refereeing Neath's 3-0 win.

Saturday, 14th January, 1967　　**Kick off 2.45 p.m.**

Neath & District Junior R.U.
0

Neath
29

G. Thomas (B F Steel)	Full Back	G. T. R. Hodgson *	15
B. Price (Metal Box)	Right Wing	H. Rees (Capt.)	14
G. Richards (Cimla)	Right Centre	G. Ball	13
R. Thomas (Neath Athletic)	Left Centre	D. B. Davies *	12
G. Watkins (Bryncoch)	Left Wing	G. Weaver	11
J. Weaver (Glynneath) Capt	Outside Half	K. Evans	10
J. Jones (Metal Box)	Inside Half	D. Parker	9
M. Prosser (Metal Box)	Forwards	J. Dodd	1
W. Jones (Cwmgwrach)		N. Rees	2
D. Cole (Cwmgwrach)		W. Williams	3
M. Williams (Metal Box)		J. Pyles	4
B. Thomas (Metal Box)		B. Davies	5
R. Thomas (Banwen)		R. Davies	6
D. Ralph (Cimla)		A. Butler	8
P. Rees (Glynneath)		M. Prosser	7

Referee : 　　　　　　　* Denotes International

NOTES.

Today's game, an extra fixture on the card, was arranged with the Neath and District Junior R.U. when Llanelli requested a postponement to keep their ground in good condition for their match with the Australians.

Neath members will see the pick of the Junior Clubs in action, and one player in particular Johnny Weaver will need no introduction to the Gnoll. We expect a bright and entertaining game.　　　　　R. D.

PEN PICTURE

DAVID PARKER.　　Aged 22　　8st. 10lb.　　5ft. 2ias.

Storage Checker at Eaglesbush Works. Came to Neath via Briton Ferry and Swansea Athletic. David is the latest member of the Parker family who have worn the "All Black" jersey, and enjoys the distinction of probably being the smallest player in first class Rugby. Interested in all types of sport, David plays cricket for Metal Box Company. Main hobby - collecting sports programmes.

Left: A fixture against the Neath & District Rugby Union traditionally provided the pipe-opener to Neath's seasons until the 1920s, but the gap between first-class and junior rugby was ever-widening. In January 1967 though, the junior union stepped in to fill a blank on the Neath list and performed creditably enough in a 0-29 defeat by the Welsh championship pace-setters.

Below: Bridgend were among the chasing pack but they were soundly thrashed 35-0 on this visit to The Gnoll. Note the brief pen-picture of Ron Waldron.

Saturday, 4th March, 1967　　**Kick off 3.15 p.m.**

Bridgend　　　　　　**Neath**

15	A. N. Other	Full Back	G. T. R. Hodgson *	15
14	Brian Coles	Right Wing	H. Rees	14
13	Ron Evans *	Right Centre	G. Ball	13
12	Geoff Davies	Left Centre	D. B. Davies *	12
11	Lyn Davies *	Left Wing	H. Williams	11
10	Keith Bradshaw *	Outside Half	K. Evans	10
9	Wynne Jones	Inside Half	M. Davies	9
1	John Lloyd (Capt.) *	Forwards	J. Dodd	1
2	Meirion Davies		M. Williams	2
3	Brian Jones		W. Williams	3
4	Boyo James		B. Thomas (Capt.) *	4
5	Terry Draper		B. Davies	5
6	Derek Brain		R. Davies	6
8	Colin Standing		A. Butler	8
7	Leighton Davies		M. Prosser	7

Referee : Mr. D. M. DAVIES (Llanrhidian)　　* Denotes International

NOTES.

We welcome our Bridgend visitors, fresh from their excellent win over Cardiff on Wednesday. Followers of both Clubs hope that today's game will emulate the one played at Brewery Field earlier this season, generally agreed to be one of the best for many years.

The twice postponed Floodlight Alliance game with Swansea will now be played on Thursday next 9th March, kick-off 7.15 p.m.

Martin Green, Cambridge University captain has informed Neath and Aberavon Committees that members of his team are involved with examinations on March 10 and 13. In view of these circumstances, both Clubs have with regret agreed to release the University from the fixtures.

We are indebted to Messrs David S. Smith Ltd. (Printers & Box Manufacturers) who have kindly borne the cost of printing today's programme.　　　　R. D.

PEN PICTURE

RON WALDRON　　Aged 31　　14st. 10lbs.　　6ft.

Steelworker at Margam works of Steel Co. of Wales. Longest serving member of the team, Ron played his first game for Neath against Rosslyn Park on 13th September, 1952. During National Service represented Royal Navy and Combined Services. Is a Glam. County player, a Barbarian and International with 4 caps, he also toured South Africa with Wales in 1964. A real family man, Ron has five children, Mark, Judith, Janet, Timothy and Lynne. Plays squash and badminton During Summer spends as much time as he can swimming and on the beach with his children. Interested in bird-watching on the Gower marshes.

Dai Morris missed the win over Bridgend as he was rested before earning the first of his 34 caps for Wales. He made his Neath debut in March 1963 in a 3–3 draw against Loughbrough Colleges alongside Jim Giddings, who was later instrumental in compiling the club's photographic collection. 'The Shadow' as Dai became known, is a legendary Neath figure. Dai Morris was one of the most perceptive rugby players ever to wear the black shirt. He had an almost supernatural ability to be wherever the ball was. Superbly fit and an instinctive reader of the game, Dai joined Neath from Glynneath and carried on playing for village side Rhigos until past his fiftieth birthday.

Neath were champions of Britain in 1966/67 and the team was awarded the *Sunday Telegraph* Pennant as the most outstanding team in these isles. Pictured are, from left to right, back row: R. Parker (Committee), S. Davies (Committee), M. Truman, G. John, J. Pyles, B. Davies, W.D. Morris, J. Dodd, H. Rees, M. Williams. Middle: N. Biggs (Coach), A. Morgan (Committee), D.B. Davies, C. Challinor (Committee), A. Butler, W. Lauder, W. Williams, M. Prosser, N. Rees, R. Waldron. Front: H.M. Powell (Committee), C. Harris (Committee), M. Davies, R. Davies (Fixture Secretary), D. Parker, R. Williams (Chairman), B. Thomas (Captain), G.T.R. Hodgson, C. Niven (Committee), K. Evans, G. Ball. Absent: H. Williams.

	P	W	D	L	F	A	%		P	W	D	L	F	A	%
Neath	44	35	2	7	594	190	81.82	Maesteg	38	20	3	15	324	289	56.58
Newbridge	38	28	4	6	530	276	78.95	Llanelli	49	24	6	19	489	421	55.10
Cardiff	46	34	3	9	656	322	77.17	Abertillery	36	17	2	17	299	285	50.00
Bridgend	49	32	2	15	669	423	67.35	Tredegar	28	11	5	12	257	229	48.21
Aberavon	47	29	5	13	428	297	67.02	Swansea	46	16	4	26	388	428	39.13
London Welsh	38	24	2	12	474	279	65.79	Cross Keys	42	14	3	25	263	423	36.90
Newport	48	28	7	13	544	344	65.63	Pontypool	50	14	4	32	290	473	32.00
Ebbw Vale	48	29	4	15	595	347	64.58	Glam. Wanderers	35	9	1	25	201	553	27.14
Pontypridd	38	21	4	13	396	265	60.53	Penarth	41	7	2	32	166	404	19.51

The final Welsh-championship table from 1966/67. Neath held off the challenge of Newbridge, whom they defeated in the only game between the clubs. The return fixture was cancelled after a Newbridge official publicly accused Neath of biting their winger Les Hewer. Neath fans, never short of humour, adapted their 'Neath, Neath, Neath' chant to 'Teeth, Teeth, Teeth'!

WESTERN MAIL, FRIDAY, APRIL 28, 1967

New Zealand style rugby pays Neath

By J. B. G. THOMAS

NEATH, the new Welsh club champions, play the game the New Zealand way. They argue it is the most effective method, and since they have won the championship, they have proved their point. They wear all-black jerseys similar to those worn by New Zealand; the only difference in their appearance is the white Maltese Cross instead of the Silver Fern.

The ultimate accolade: not for nothing are Neath known as the 'Welsh All Blacks'!

DATE 1966	FIXTURE LIST, 1966-67	Gr'nd	Res't	NEATH G	T	P	OPPONENT G	T	P
Sept 3	Pontypridd	Home	W		9			3	
10	Ebbw Vale	Home	W		25			3	
15	Cross Keys	Home	W		22				
17	Newport	Away	W						
24	Maesteg	Away	W		12				
Oct. 1	Llanelly	Home	W		11				
3	Penarth	Away							
8	Aberavon	Home	W		31				
15	Pontypool	Away	W		15				
18	Cardiff T.C. (F/Lights)	Home	W		11				
22	Swansea	Away	W		6				
29	*Neath & Aberavon v. Australia at Neath	–	L		3		3		
Nov. 2	Bridgend	Away	W		15				
5	Bath	Away	W		15				
12	Newbridge	Home	W		19				
19	Penarth	Home	W		17				
26	Blackheath	Home	W		10				
Dec. 3	Gloucester	Away	W		9				
10	Pontypool	Home	W		14				
17	Cardiff	Away	W		6				
24	London Welsh	Home	W		5				
26	Aberavon	Away	W		6				
31	Swansea	Home	L						
1967									
Jan. 7	Coventry	Home	W		5			3	
14	Llanelly	Away							
21	Final Trial at Swansea	–							
26	Oxford (F/Lights)	–	W		27			0	
28	Barbarians v. Australia	C'diff							
Feb. 1	Loughborough C.(F/L)	Home	W						
4	Newbridge	Away	W		6				
6	Cardiff (F/Lights)	Home	W		9				
11	Maesteg	Home	W						
18	Aberavon	Away	L		3				
25	London Welsh	Away	W		35				
Mar. 4	Bridgend	Home	L						
6	Cross Keys	Away	W						
11	Wales v. Ireland	C'diff							
13	*Cambridge University	Home			6				
18	Ebbw Vale	Away	L		14				
25	St. Luke's College	Home	W						
27	Aberavon	Home	W		25				
April 1	Richmond	Home	W		17				
6	Swansea	Away	W		27				
8	Gloucester	Home	W		6				
13	Llanelly	Home							
15	Wales v. England	C'diff							
22	Newport	Home	W		3			0	
25	Pontypridd	Away	W		12			9	
29	Welsh Seven-a-Side	–							

*Membership Ticket will not admit holder to this match

Neath RFC season ticket for 1966/67 belonging to Mr D. Malcolm Thomas (a leading Neath antiquarian), who thoughtfully recorded the season's results for posterity. Neath played a further 10 fixtures not on the season ticket. These resulted in wins against Briton Ferry (35-0), Skewen (22-0), Neath & District RU (29-0), Llanelli (13-0), Swansea (13-6) and Aberavon Green Stars (12-8). There was also a loss at Aberavon (0-6) in the Floodlight Alliance competition. The Blacks also toured Jersey, winning two games 25-0 and 43-0, and they beat an International XV 40-20.

ARTHUR'S RECORD—AND IT WAS ALMOST OVERLOOKED!

By Trevor Dargavel

NEATH'S Arthur Griffiths is now the longest-serving secretary in Welsh rugby. And this remarkable record — he's in his 38th year — has almost been overlooked in a year when Neath have had so much success and more than their share of controversy.

He even worked as an officer from long range when a Civil Service posting took him from his home town for a short period.

For that short time he was forced to vacate the general secretary's chair, but otherwise he has held the office since 1930.

Previously he had acted as assistant secretary and before that began a long association with Neath as secreatary of the Supporters' Club.

HOT LINE

Mr. Griffiths, whose telephone has been busier than ever over the past year, admits that the period has been one of the most troublesome during his long period in office.

And that's some admission. For like any good secretary, he has lost count of the number of problems he has been called upon to iron out in the normal running of the club during an administrative career which now extends to well over a third of the club's history.

With telephone inquiries alone over the past year, some connected with suc-

cesses and others with controversial issues, Mr. Griffiths must have been more than harassed.

But through it all, he has used his great experience to maintain an outward calm and any enquirer has always been assured of the utmost courtesy.

And courtesy was the key note in last week's match with Cardiff. I doubt whether there could possibly have been any cause for complaint over proceedings on or off the field. The next move, whatever that might be, is awaited.

The hope in many quarters even outside the respective clubs involved in the controversy, is that some way can be found to arrange round the table talks to arrange settlement of a dispute which has had a marring effect upon the Welsh club scene throughout this season.

● ARTHUR GRIFFITHS . . . it's been his busiest season

In September 1967, the *South Wales Evening Post* paid tribute to the long service of secretary Arthur Griffiths.

Left: Arthur Griffiths.

Below: Rees Stephens was elected to the Welsh Rugby Union in 1962 and soon became a national selector. Here, the 'Big Five' of 1966/67 are in discussion: Rees Stephens, Glyn Morgan, Cliff Jones, Harry Bowcott and Alun Thomas.

Right: The 1967/68 season kicked off controversially when Randall Davies was sent off at Cardiff in September. It is alleged that the Neath cry that went out from the kick-off was 'Charge!', and fixtures were temporarily cancelled between the two clubs. The suspension of fixtures captured national headlines and provoked this cartoon by 'Jon'.

Below: Brian Lochore's 1967/68 All Blacks played West Wales at Swansea on 8 November 1967. Six Neath men played an important role as the regional XV (minus the services of four Welsh internationals) took on the mighty New Zealanders and battled bravely in a 14-21 defeat. Long-striding Neath winger Hywel Williams, a teacher in Cardigan, got the West Wales try.

NEW ZEALAND All Black		Referee: M. H. Titcombe (R.F.U.) Bristol		WEST WALES XV Red jerseys, White shorts, Red and White hooped stockings
BRIAN JAMES LOCHORE *The New Zealand Captain*				CLIVE ROWLANDS *The West Wales XV Captain*
21 G. F. KEMBER (WELLINGTON)		FULL BACKS		15 D. REES (SWANSEA)
26 P. H. CLARKE (MARLBOROUGH)	RIGHT WING	THREE-QUARTERS	RIGHT WING	14 H. REES (NEATH)
23 W. D. COTTRELL (CANTERBURY)	RIGHT CENTRE		RIGHT CENTRE	13 J. DAVIES (SWANSEA)
24 G. S. THORNE (AUCKLAND)	LEFT CENTRE		LEFT CENTRE	12 C. JONES (ABERAVON)
27 A. G. STEEL (CANTERBURY)	LEFT WING		LEFT WING	11 H. WILLIAMS (NEATH)
20 M. A. HEREWINI (AUCKLAND)	OUTSIDE HALF	HALF-BACKS	OUTSIDE HALF	10 J. K. EVANS (NEATH)
17 S. M. GOING (NORTH AUCKLAND)	INSIDE HALF		INSIDE HALF	9 *D. C. T. ROWLANDS (Capt.) (SWANSEA)
2 K. F. GRAY (WELLINGTON)		FORWARDS		1 R. B. GALE (LLANELLI)
3 J. MAJOR (TARANAKI)				2 R. THOMAS (SWANSEA)
6 A. E. HOPKINSON (CANTERBURY)				3 W. WILLIAMS (NEATH)
11 A. G. JENNINGS (BAY OF PLENTY)				4 B. DAVIES (NEATH)
8 C. E. MEADS (Capt.) (KING C'TRY)				5 *W. D. THOMAS (LLANELLI)
7 M. C. WILLS (TARANAKI)				6 *D. MORRIS (NEATH)
14 I. A. KIRKPATRICK (CANTERB'Y)				8 R. WANBON (ABERAVON)
12 K. R. TREMAIN (HAWKES BAY)				7 M. EVANS (SWANSEA)

Touch Judge:
W. D. H. Davies (W.R.U.) Ystalyfera

Touch Judge:
D. G. Swain (W.R.U.) Carmarthen

* INTERNATIONALS

Neath RFC 1968/69, captained by centre Glen Ball, one of the club's finest-ever centres, who was unfortunate to miss out on full Wales honours, although he did play two 'Tests' for Wales in the uncapped games in Argentina in 1968. His side's record read: Played 48, Won 28, Drew 1, Lost 19, Points For 628, Points Against 420. Grahame Hodgson scored 159 points with Martyn Davies and Dai Morris scoring 16 tries apiece. From left to right, back row: A. Hughes, M. Shore, B. Davies, J. Pyles, W. Williams, J. Roberts. Standing: W. Davies, A. Mages, W.D. Morris, M. Truman, B. Thomas, D. Thomas, M. Prosser. Seated: D. Jenkins, D. Parker, C. Harris (Chairman), G. Ball (Captain), M. Davies, G.T.R. Hodgson, H. Williams.

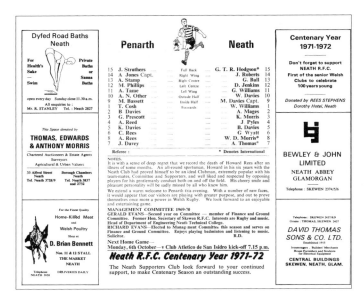

Popular winger Howard Rees joined Neath from BP Llandarcy in 1963, but he died at a tragically young age in September 1969. Fixture secretary Ron Davies paid tribute to a worthy All Black in his programme notes for the next home game against Penarth on 2 October 1969.

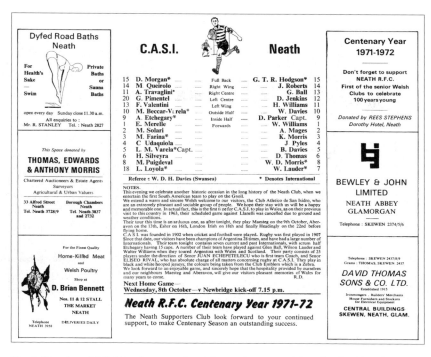

On 6 October 1969 Neath entertained Argentine opposition for the first time, beating Club Atletico de San Isidro (CASI) 13-6.

Neath finished third in the Welsh championship in 1969/70. Their record was: Played 41, Won 29, Drawn 4, Lost 8, Points For 600, Points Against 319. Grahame Hodgson scored 184 points and John Roberts (nephew of Cyril) got 21 tries. From left to right, back row: M. Thomas, A. Morgan, B. Dennis, A. Benjamin, G. Evans, N. Biggs, E. Case, C. Niven, M.L. Thomas, G. Ball. Standing: R. Waldron, J. Roberts, W. Williams, W. Pritchard, B. Davies, B. Thomas, S. Hodgson, G. Shaw, K. Morris, D. Thomas, W. Lauder, R. Parker. Seated: G. Jones, C. Challinor, R. Williams, R. Davies, M. Davies (Captain), T. Lodge (Chairman), D. Parker, H. Morris, S. Davies, H. Powell, C. Harris. Front: J. McAvoy, K. Collier, W. Davies, G.T.R. Hodgson.

Neath won the Snelling Sevens again in 1970. Pictured are, from left to right: Glen Ball, Wynne Davies (kneeling), John Roberts, Wilson Lauder, Dai Parker, Norman Rees, Dai Morris.

Dai Parker, one of the smallest men to play top-class rugby, won the Bill Everson Player of the Tournament award. Parker shared the scrum-half role at The Gnoll with Martyn Davies but, to accommodate both in the same team, later switched to outside half with considerable success.

A West German XV   Neath

15	Schnell*	Full Back	G. T. R. Hodgson*	15
14	Gerling	Right Wing	J Roberts	14
13	Wohler*	Right Centre	G. Ball	13
12	Nowack*	Left Centre	D. Jenkins	12
11	Walter	Left Wing	Owen Jones	11
10	Creutz	Outside Half	W. Davies	10
9	Selligmall*	Inside Half	M. Davies (Capt.)	9
1	Marach*	Forwards	W. Williams	1
2	Schmidt* (Capt.)		A. J. Mages	2
3	Flohr*		J. Pyles	3
4	Rolke*		B. Davies	4
5	Hoppe*		Brian Thomas *	5
6	Morgenroth*		M. Thomas	6
8	Dorr*		W. D. Morris*	8
7	Kotte*		Wilson Lauder*	7

Referee :   Mr. W. K. M. JONES (Llanelli)   Denotes International

NOTES.

Neath R.F.C. embarks upon season 1970/71 (the 99th in the long history of the Club),
with high hopes and ambitions, — — as proud holders of the "Snelling Sevens" Cup,
and among the top three Clubs in last year's unofficial Welsh Championship. To new
Club Chairman Norman Biggs, his Officials & Committee, and team, once again
captained by Martyn Davies, we wish a happy and successful season both on and off
the field.

This evening marks a further event in the Club's history with the first visit of yet
another foreign rugby playing nation, and we extend the warmest of Welsh welcomes
to our visitors from West Germany to the famous Gnoll Ground.

German rugby has not received much publicity in this country, yet their records show
that rugby has been played in Germany since 1872.

The German Rugby Federation was founded in 1900, and its present President Herr
Heinz Reinhold who has held office since 1956, is accompanying our visitors this
evening.

There are over 80 Clubs in the German Rugby Federation and in common with other
countries much encouragement is being given to Youth Rugby.

Germany is a member of the F.I.R.A. and has been playing other nations such as
France 'B', Italy, Rumania, Poland, Spain and Czechoslovakia over the years.   The
German XV last toured this country in 1966 when they played Llanelli, Cardiff and Bath.
Captaining the side is H. Schmidt who has been "capped" 21 times.

R. D.

Next Home Game—Saturday, 5th September
v. NUNEATON   K.O. 3.15 p.m.

Above: Neath enjoyed their first victory
over a national side on 3 September 1970
when they defeated West Germany 28-0
at The Gnoll. On the left wing for Neath
was R.O.P. (Owen) Jones, an Amman
Valley GS product who kicked Oxford
University to victory in the 1970 Varsity
Match. Jones was a student teacher at
Neath Grammar School and later became
headmaster of Cwrt Sart CS, then
Amman Valley CS, and was one of
Wales' leading referees.

Right: Since the Second World War,
Neath occasionally hosted games against
the West Wales Rugby Union, a red-hot
breeding ground for future All Blacks.

W.W.R.U.   Neath

15	John Howells (Penclawdd)	Full Back	G.T.R. Hodgson*	15
14	Dyfrig Powell (Tumble)	Right Wing	G. Williams	14
13	Mel Leach (Llandybie)	Right Centre	G. Ball	13
12	David Prendiville (Felinfoel)	Left Centre	D. Lewis	12
11	Carwyn Thomas (Amman Utd)	Left Wing	H. Williams	11
10	Keith Evans (Cwmgors)	Outside Half	D. Hoare	10
9	Ellis Wyn Williams (Brynamman)	Inside Half	M. Davies Capt.	9
1	Paul Jones (Penclawdd)	Forwards	W. Williams	1
2	Geoffrey Davies (Felinfoel)		A. Mages	2
3	Richard Conway (Tumble)		D. Jones	3
4	Henry Allen (Crynant)		J. Pyles	4
5	Griff Evans (Seven Sisters)		B. Davies	5
6	Ron Jones Capt. (Vardre Utd)		A. Thomas*	6
8	Rowley Phillips (Llandybie)		G. Wyatt	8
7	Clive Lewis (Abercrave)		D. Thomas	7

Referee : Mr. D. G. WATTS (Llandybie)   * Denotes International

NOTES.

Due to the President's Croeso Celebrations Match being played at Cardiff tomorrow,
we stage our first official fixture of the season 1969/70 this evening.

We extend a cordial welcome to the West Wales R. U. whose team contains a number
of well known players, among them being former Neath fly-half Keith Evans.

The Neath team contains some new names, and we wish them a successful debut in
the "All Black" colours.

Congratulations to our summer counterparts Neath Cricket Club on once again
winning the Championship of the South Wales Cricket League.

MANAGEMENT COMMITTEE 1969-70

CYRIL NIVEN (Chairman)—Has been a member of Committee for 12 years, during
which time he has served on all the various sub-
committees of the Club.   Main interests are Rugby and
gardening.   Foreman at Steel Co. of Wales, Margam.

Next Home Game—
Saturday, 13th September—v Bective Rangers kick-off 3.15 p.m.

Neath R.F.C. Centenary Year 1971-72

The Neath Supporters Club look forward to your continued
support, to make Centenary Season an outstanding success.

Neath RFC 1970/71 won 29, drew 4 and lost 15 of their 48 games, scoring 760 points and conceding 373. John Roberts equalled his Uncle Cyril's best with 27 tries, while flanker Mike Thomas (a Neath Colts product who led Swansea RFC in 1966/67) scored a record for a forward of 23 tries. Tragedy was to strike this side too, for promising prop Keith Morris (back row, third left) was to break his neck while coaching schoolboys in Brecon. From left to right, back row: W. Davies, D. Jenkins, K. Morris, B. Thomas, W. Williams, E. Staton, D. Thomas. Standing: R. Arbourne, G. Ball, G. Jarvis, W.D. Morris, G. Shaw, W. Pritchard, B. Davies, W. Lauder, A. Hughes. Seated: M. Thomas, D. Parker, M. Davies (Captain), N. Biggs (Coach), G.T.R. Hodgson, J. Roberts, J. McAvoy.

Neath Rugby Football Club Captains

★

1871-72	Dr. T. P. Whittington		1926-27	D. Pascoe and Dan Jones
1872-84	No records kept		1927-28	G. Edwards
1884-85	A. T. Williams		1928-29	T. Evans
1885-86	S. S. Clarke		1929-30	T. Evans
1886-87	S. S. Clarke		1930-31	T. Hollingdale
1887-88	S. S. Clarke		1931-32	T. Arthur
1888-89	H. A. Bowen		1932-33	G. Hopkins
1889-90	Dr. H. V. Pegge		1933-34	A. Hickman
1890-91	Dr. H. V. Pegge		1934-35	Glyn Daniels
1891-92	Dr. H. V. Pegge		1935-36	Gwyn Moore
1892-93	G. D. Trick		1936-37	H. Thomas
1893-94	G. D. Trick		1937-38	D. L. Thomas
1894-95	C. Steer		1938-39	W. E. Jones
1895-96	C. Steer		1939-40	A. McCarley (elected)
1896-97	W. Jones		1940-45	War
1897-98	W. Jones		1945-46	Tom James
1898-99	W. Jones		1946-47	C. Williams
1899-1900	Joe Davies		1947-48	Viv Evans
1900-01	W. Jones		1948-49	Morlais Thomas
1901-02	W. Jones		1949-50	H. Edwards
1902-03	D. H. Davies		1950-51	Roy John
1903-04	Howell Jones		1951-52	Rees Stephens
1904-05	Howell Jones		1952-53	Rees Stephens
1905-06	W. Jones		1953-54	Rees Stephens
1906-07	W. Jones		1954-55	Gareth Thomas
1907-08	W. Jones		1955-56	D. T. Meredith
1908-09	W. Jones		1957-58	Keith Maddocks
1909-10	Frank Rees		1958-59	D. B. Rees
1910-11	Frank Rees		1959-60	R. Waldron
1911-12	W. J. Perry		1960-61	J. Dodd
1912-13	F. David		1961-62	J. Dodd
1913-14	T. C. Lloyd		1962-63	M. Williams
1914-15	J. Pulman (elected)		1963-64	J. Dodd
1915-19	War		1964-65	G. T. R. Hodgson
1919-20	W. Hopkins		1965-66	R. Thomas
1920-21	L. Gwyn Thomas		1966-67	B. Thomas
1921-22	R. V. Hill		1967-68	B. Thomas
1922-23	J. Jones		1968-69	G. Ball
1923-24	Ivor Jones		1969-70	Martyn Davies
1924-25	D. Hiddlestone		1970-71	Martyn Davies
1925-26	Jim John		1971-72	Martyn Davies

This is a copy of the Captains Board which was presented to the Neath Club by the Supporters' Club. Research was carried out by Mr. W. Ivor Davies, who also carried out research into the club's history. His assistance is appreciated.

Neath RFC captains – the first 100 years!

Above: The Neath squad that set out in 1971/72 ,when Neath became the first of the senior Welsh clubs to celebrate its centenary, the first recorded match having been played at Swansea in February 1872. From left to right, standing: N. Biggs, C. Harris, R.J. Trimnell, T. Dargavel, A. Morgan, K. Morris, W. Lauder, W.D. Morris, J.C. Bewley, W. Williams, B. Thomas, W. Pritchard, B. Davies, G. Shaw, E. Case, J.D. Bevan, B. Dennis, A. Meredith, A. Morris, G. Jones, R. Parker, S. Davies, J.R.G. Stephens. Seated: C. Challinor, D. Thomas, R. Williams, G.T.R. Hodgson, T. Lodge, M. Davies (Captain), R.B. Jones, J. Roberts, R. Davies, N. Rees, H.M. Powell. Front: W. Davies, D. Parker, D. Jenkins, G. Ball.

Opposite left: Scrum-half Martyn Davies captained Neath during their centenary season when the All Blacks became the first senior Welsh club to celebrate 100 years in existence. Apart from being the first captain to hold aloft the new WRU Cup, Martyn Davies was one of the most accomplished scrum-workers in Wales and gained Wales 'B' and Barbarians honours. He led Neath for four seasons from 1969/70 to 1972/73 with Dai Parker as his deputy. A head teacher at Bryncoch, Martyn later served as committee man and coach of Neath RFC and still holds the club appearance record with 511.

Opposite right: The Author's season ticket for the centenary season.

1971 - 1972

NEATH RUGBY
FOOTBALL CLUB

CENTENARY SEASON

Boy's
Season Ticket

The crowning moment of Neath's centenary year. From left to right: N. Rees, W. Williams, G. Shaw, J. Poole, W. Davies, B. Davies, B. Thomas, M. Davies (Captain), M. Thomas, W. Lauder, D. Parker, D. Jenkins, G. Ball, K. Collier (hidden), C. Harris (Committee), W.D. Morris, C. Challinor (Committee).

The Neath RFC Players' Society was launched in 1971/72 with the following committee, five of whom had played pre-war: from left to right, back row: J. Dodd, E.R. John, D.T. Meredith, T.O. Jones, R. Waldron, R. Thomas. Seated: H.M. Powell, R. Davies (Secretary), J.R.G. Stephens (Chairman), C. Challinor, C. Harris, E.C. Roberts.

The Supporters' Club issued this handy fixture booklet for the centenary season.

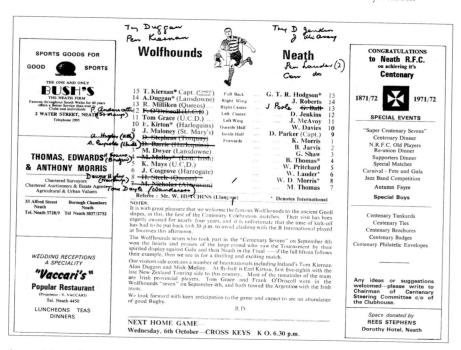

A prestigious fixture for Neath was a visit from the Irish Wolfhounds, who found themselves a man short, so Neath prop Alan Hughes (who had played for Neath Athletic earlier that afternoon) stepped in to play his second game in a day. Hooker Arwyn Reynolds, lock Howard Evans and No. 8 Dennis Hughes joined him in the elite band of Welshmen to have represented the famous Wolfhounds.

Barbarians 12   Neath 4

Barbarians			Neath
15	A. M. Jorden Blackheath (England) 2 CONV.	Full Back	G. T. R. Hodgson (Wales) 15
14	I. Hall Aberavon (Wales)	Right Wing	K. Collier 14
13	R. A. Milliken Queen's University, Belfast	Right Centre	G. Ball 13
12	K. S. Hughes London Welsh (Wales)	Left Centre	D. Jenkins 12
11	B. P. Bulpitt Blackheath	Left Wing	TRY J. McAvoy 11
10	I. D. Wright Northampton (England) TRY	Outside Half	W. Davies 10
9	I. G. McCrae Gordonians (Scotland) TRY	Inside Half	D. Parker (Capt.) 9
1	D. B. Llewellyn Llanelli (Wales)	Forwards	I. Wagstaffe 1
2	D. M. Barry (Harlequins)		G. Jarvis 2
3	D. L. Powell Northampton (England) CAPTAIN		B. Thomas G. Shaw 3
4	M. G. Molloy London Irish (Ireland)		W. Pritchard 4
5	C. W. Ralston Richmond (England)		B. Davies B. Thomas (Wales) 5
6	A. L. Bucknell Richmond (England)		W. Lauder (Scotland) 6
8	P. Dixon Harlequins (England)		W. D. Morris (Wales) 8
7	A. J. Grey London Welsh (Wales)		D. Thomas 7

Referee : Mr. MEIRION JOSEPH (Hitchin)

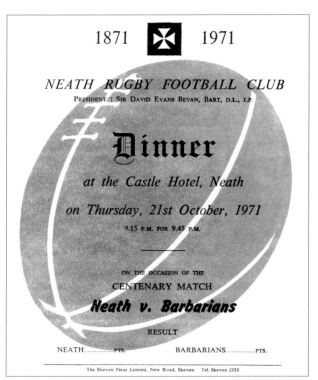

1871   1971

NEATH RUGBY FOOTBALL CLUB

PRESIDENT : SIR DAVID EVANS BEVAN, BART, D.L., J.P.

Dinner

at the Castle Hotel, Neath

on Thursday, 21st October, 1971

9.15 P.M. FOR 9.45 P.M.

ON THE OCCASION OF THE

CENTENARY MATCH

Neath v. Barbarians

RESULT

NEATH............PTS.   BARBARIANS............PTS.

The Skewen Press Limited, New Road, Skewen   Tel. Skewen 2353

Above: Among the many special centenary fixtures, Neath hosted the Barbarians for the fourth time in October 1971. The Ba-Bas' three previous visits had been in the early 1920s, but this time they earned their first win at The Gnoll 12-4, thanks to tries by halves Ian Wright and Gordon McCrae, both converted by Tony Jorden, against a sole try by Jeff McAvoy for Neath.

Left: The dinner menu from the post-match function at the Castle Hotel, birthplace of the WRU in 1881.

A Snelling "Sevens" Menu

LLANELLI MUSHROOM SOUP
OR
SWANSEA FRUIT JUICE

NEATH ROAST BEEF
ABERAVON HORSERADISH SAUCE
MAESTEG ROAST POTATOES
BRIDGEND BOILED POTATOES
GLAMORGAN WANDERERS GARDEN PEAS
PENARTH CAULIFLOWER
PONTYPRIDD CARROTS

CARDIFF APPLE PIE
NEWPORT FRESH CREAM

EBBW VALE ASSORTED CHEESES
ABERTILLERY ROLLS
PONTYPOOL BISCUITS
CROSS KEYS BUTTER

NEWBRIDGE COFFEE

Toast List

GRACE

"HER MAJESTY THE QUEEN"
THE CHAIRMAN

"THE BARBARIANS"

Proposer : RALPH WILLIAMS Esq.
Chairman Centenary Steering Committee Neath R.F.C.

Response : Brigadier H. L. GLYN HUGHES, C.B.E.
President Barbarians R.F.C.

"NEATH R.F.C."

Proposer : HERBERT WADDELL Esq.
Vice-President Barbarians R.F.C.

Response : R. B. JONES Esq.
Chairman, Neath Rugby Football Club

Note the 'Snelling' menu ranging from Llanelli mushroom soup to Newbridge coffee.

THE MAYOR OF NEATH
(Councillor E. J. G. HEMMING)
requests the honour of the Company of

Mr Ron Davies

at the
CIVIC CENTRE, NEATH, ON FRIDAY, 26TH NOVEMBER, 1971,
at 3.0 p.m., on the occasion of the Presentation of the
HONORARY FREEDOM OF THE BOROUGH
TO
NEATH RUGBY FOOTBALL CLUB

R.S.V.P. to the Town Clerk, Neath, on enclosed
Card not later than 19th November, 1971.

Please bring this invitation with you as
Card of Admission to Ceremony.

On Friday 26 November 1971, Neath RFC became the first organisation to be granted the Honorary Freedom of the Borough of Neath by the Mayor, Councillor E.J.G. (Gerry) Hemming, who had reported the Welsh All Blacks' deeds for many years for the *Neath Guardian*. This invitation card belonged to fixture-secretary Ron Davies, who was acting secretary for the centenary season due to the illness of long-serving Arthur Griffiths.

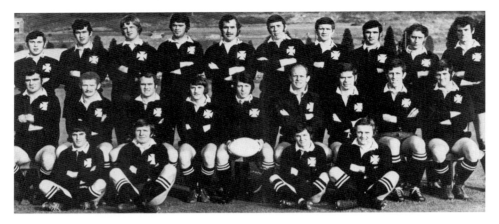

Neath RFC 1971/72, centenary season. From left to right, back row: J. Poole,
D.R. Thomas, R. Hughes, S. Hodgson, B. Thomas, B. Davies, G. Shaw, P. Langford,
K. Collier, W.D. Morris. Seated: W. Williams, K. Morris, N. Rees, D. Davies, M. Davies
(Captain), G.T.R. Hodgson, G. Ball, W. Lauder, D. Thomas. Front: J. McAvoy,
M. Thomas, D. Parker, D. Jenkins.

Neath played a strong WRU President's XV in April 1972. The select side
included two 'foreign' Lions stars in Coventry winger David Duckham (an
adopted Welshman following his try-scoring exploits in New Zealand in 1971)
and Scotland lock Gordon Brown. Due to injuries, Neath played flanker Mike
Thomas on the wing. It was 5 tries apiece, but the President's XV won 31-26
through tries by John Taylor (2), Duckham, Ron Evans (an ex-Neath outside
half) and Ian Hall, with conversions by Evans, Taylor, Brown and Gareth
Edwards, who also kicked a penalty. Neath's points came via tries by Ken
Collier (2), David Jenkins, Richard Thomas (later Cambridge University and
London Welsh) and Wilson Lauder, who converted 3.

Menu

Soup and Bread Rolls

———

Roast Turkey & Seasoning
Creamed Potatoes
Cauliflower or Sprouts
Garden Peas
Buttered Carrots

———

Fruit Salad & Cream
Sherry Trifles
or Peaches & Cream

———

Cheese & Biscuits

———

Coffee

———

Half Bottle of Wine per person

Toast List

GRACE

by

Mr. Ron Davies, Hon. General Secretary of
Neath R.F.C.

———

THE QUEEN

Proposed by

Mr. Rees Stephens J.P., Chairman of the Neath R.F.C. Players Society

———

NEATH R.F.C. PLAYERS SOCIETY

Proposed by

Mr. Rhys E. Williams, President of the Welsh Rugby Union
and
Councillor Gerald D. Hemming, His Worship the Mayor of Neath

Response by
Mr. Martyn Davies, Captain of Neath R.F.C.

———

THE GUEST SPEAKER

Mr. J.B.G. Thomas, Sports Editor, Western Mail

Introduced by
Mr. R.B. Jones, Chairman of Neath R.F.C.

Above: The menu card from the inaugural dinner of the Neath RFC Players' Society. Among the speakers were WRU president Rhys Emlyn Williams (from nearby Crynant), Mayor Gerry Hemming and Welsh rugby writer J.B.G. Thomas.

Right: The programme from the first WRU Cup final played at the National Stadium on 6 May 1972.

	Kick-off 3 p.m.		**LLANELLI** (Red Jerseys)		**NEATH** (Black Jerseys)
Full Backs (CEFNWR)		15	R. Davies	15	W. Davies
Right Wing (Asgell dde)		14	A. Hill	14	K. Collier
Right Centre (Canolwr)		13	B. Fowler	13	G. Ball
Left Centre (Canolwr)		12	R. Gravelle	12	D. Jenkins
Left Wing (Asgell chwith)		11	R. Mathias	11	J. Poole
Stand off (Maswr)		10	P. Bennett	10	D. Parker
Scrum-half (Mewnwr)		9	S. Williams	9	M. Davies (Capt.)
Prop (Y rheng flaen)		1	A. Crocker	1	W. Williams
Hooker (Bachwr)		2	R. Thomas	2	R. Thomas N. Rees
Prop (Y rheng flaen)		3	D. B. Llewelyn (Capt.)	3	G. Shaw
Lock (Yr ail reng)		4	W. D. Thomas	4	B. Thomas
Lock (Yr ail reng)		5	D. Quinnell	5	B. Davies
Flanker (Blaenasgell)		6	A. James	6	W. Lauder
No. 8 (Y rheng ol)		8	H. Jenkins	8	D. Morris
Flanker (Blaenasgell)		7	C. John	7	M. Thomas

Referee: **M. Joseph**   Touch Judges: **E. M. Lewis and R. Lewis**

Above: Neath defeated Llanelli in the first-ever final to cap their centenary season in 1971/72. Neath played all away games on route to the final, winning at Cefneithin (15-9), Glynneath (7-3), Beddau (15-6) and Ebbw Vale (10-0) before defeating favourites Cardiff (Barry John, Gareth Edwards et al) at the Brewery Field.

Right: A celebration dinner was held at Bindles, Barry in honour of Neath (cup winners) and London Welsh (Champions).

Below right: The club's official statistics distributed at the AGM suggested that Neath had won the championship, not the cup, in 1971/72. The Blacks might well have done so had it not been for a disastrous late run that saw them win only the cup semi-final against Cardiff and the final against Llanelli as end-of-season fatigue caught up with them. In all, Neath played a record 57 games and 36 were won, 5 drawn and 16 lost. Neath employed some fifty-four players over that hectic programme, Wilson Lauder contributing 237 points and Ken Collier bagging 19 tries.

Opposite below: Neath RFC, inaugural winners of the WRU Cup, Saturday 6 May 1972. The first cup winners are pictured prior to the final at Cardiff Arms Park. 12,000 people watched the game, which netted gate receipts of £6,000! A far cry from future cup finals when Neath would pack the old National Stadium and establish new crowd records for club matches. From left to right, standing: W. Davies, W. Williams, G. Shaw, B. Thomas, B. Davies, W. Lauder, N. Rees, W.D. Morris, H.M. Powell (Team Secretary). Seated: K. Collier, J. Poole, R.B. Jones (Chairman), M. Davies (Captain), R. Davies (Secretary), D. Parker, D. Jenkins. Front: G. Ball, M. Thomas.

CELEBRATION DINNER

in honour of

LONDON WELSH R.F.C.

Leaders of the Western Mail Table 1971-72

NEATH R.F.C.

Winners of the Welsh Rugby Union Challenge Cup 1972

given by the

Chairman and Directors

of

Welsh Brewers LTD

Friday, 16th June 1972
Bindles Banqueting Suite, The Knap, Nr. Barry

Neath Rugby Football Club
(President: Sir David Evans Bevan, Bart., D.L., J.P.)

✠ ✠

Centenary Year 1971 - 1972

Welsh Rugby Union Championship Winners 1972

Played 57   Won 36   Drawn 5   Lost 16
Points for—884   Points Against—543

Player	Appearances	Tries	Conversions	Penalties	Drop Goals	Total
6. T. R. HODGSON	33	3				
W. DAVIES	34	5	6	1	3	36
J. ROBERTS	7	4				20
K. COLLIER	40	19				76
M. JENKINS	4	3				12
S. ROPER	6	1				4
G. BALL	30	2				8
D. JENKINS	30	15				60
J. McAVOY	42	11				44
J. POOLE	37	5	18	24		128
I. HOPKINS	10	1				4
D. DAVIES	9	4				16
P. GRIFFITHS	19				1	3
D. PARKER	28	2			2	14
A. JONES	4					
M. DAVIES	45	11				44
A. MEREDITH	4					
D. THOMAS	32	3				12
M. THOMAS	46	8				32
W. LAUDER	45	13	43	33		237
D. MORRIS	46	13				52
BRIAN THOMAS	30	1				4
B. DAVIES	31					
R. THOMAS	7	2				8
S. HODGSON	16	2				8
G. SHAW	45	2				8
N. REES	45	1				4
W. WILLIAMS	30	3	1			14
K. MORRIS	32	1				4
F. LANGFORD	12					
G. JARVIS	9	1				
R. HUGHES	4					
W. PRITCHARD	13	1				4
J. BEVAN	1					
M. ANTHONY	1					
W. BOWEN	1					
I. WAGSTAFF	3	1				4
N. MORGAN	1					
A. MILLARD	1					
J. PYLES	5					
F. GIBBINS	1	1				4
C. SCHUBERT	1					
A. JENKINS	1					
T. ROBERTS	1					
G. WYATT	2					
G. THOMAS	3					
R. WILLIAMS	1					
P. DENNIS	1					
B. HODGE	1					
J. HERDMAN	2					
C. BEYNON	1					
M. WILLIAMS	2					
E. O'SHEA	1					
B. EVANS	2					
Penalty Tries		1				4
TOTALS		139	68	58	6	884

Including Welsh Cup and Floodlight Alliance

83

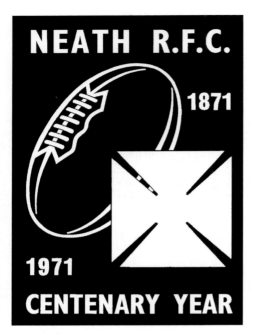

Above: Among the many 'centenary specials' was the production of a brochure by Trevor Dargavel (*Evening Post*) and Elfed Rees (*Neath Guardian*) with cover design by the ubiquitous Haydn Ford, whose caricatures adorn many a local clubhouse.

Right: The centenary season playing record.

NEATH RUGBY FOOTBALL CLUB

SEASON 1971/72		CAPTAIN - MARTYN DAVIES			
Sept.	4 Super Centenary Sevens	W			H
	8 Penarth	W	60	0	H
	11 Abertillery	W	17	6	A
	15 Cardiff	L	12	13	A
	18 Newport	W	49	16	H
	22 West Wales R.U.	W	34	7	A
	25 Wolfhounds	W	16	7	H
Oct.	2 Llanelli	L	3	19	A
	6 Cross Keys	W	36	6	H
	9 Aberavon	W	16	15	A
	16 Swansea	W	24	13	H
	21 Barbarians	L	4	12	H
	23 London Welsh	L	18	26	H
	27 Llanelli (Fl.All.)	D	8	8	A
	30 Bath	W	15	7	H
Nov.	6 Pontypool	W	27	6	A
	10 Llanelli	L	6	10	H
	13 Cefneithin (WRU Cup)	W	13	9	A
	17 Cross Keys (Fl.All.)	D	16	16	A
	20 Saracens	W	12	9	A
	24 Bridgend	W	9	6	H
	27 Blackheath	W	16	3	H
Dec.	4 Newbridge	W	18	9	A
	8 Maesteg (Fl.All.)	W	20	4	H
	11 Bridgend	W	14	4	A
	18 Ebbw Vale	W	30	4	H
	21 Glynneath (WRU Cup)	W	7	3	A
	27 Aberavon	D	7	7	H
Jan.	1 Coventry	D	13	13	A
	8 South Wales Police	W	21	13	H
	12 Cross Keys	C			A
	17 Pontypridd	W	12	0	H
	20 Beddau (WRU Cup)	W	12	6	A
	22 Nuneaton	W	9	4	A
	26 Abertillery	W	30	0	H
	29 Newport	L	7	16	A
Feb.	7 Maesteg	W	14	7	H
	12 Ebbw Vale	L	0	6	A
	19 Aberavon	D	3	3	H
	26 London Welsh	L	7	12	A
Mar.	1 Snelling XV	C			H
	4 Pontypool	W	3	0	H
	9 Maesteg	W	13	3	A
	11 Moseley	W	10	9	H
	13 Penarth	W	13	4	A
	18 Newbridge	W	29	9	H
	22 Pontypridd	L	6	9	A
	27 Ebbw Vale (WRU Cup)	W	10	0	A
	29 Swansea	W	22	4	H
Apr.	1 St. Luke's College	W	16	14	H
	3 Aberavon	L	3	0	A
	6 Llanelli	L	0	6	H
	8 Bristol	L	8	21	H
	12 Cardiff (WRU Cup S/F at Bridgend)	W	16	9	
	15 Richmond	L	15	25	A
	17 Cardiff	L	13	17	H
	19 WRU President's XV	L	30	31	H
	22 Swansea	L	4	22	A
	29 Snelling Sevens				
May	6 Llanelli (WRU Cup Final at Cardiff)	W	15	9	

INAUGURAL WINNERS OF THE WRU CUP

eight

Give it to Elgan!

Above left: Having won the cup in 1972, Neath started 1972/73 with a bang and led the Welsh championship in November, but injuries and retirements spiralled them into a long period of constant rebuilding. Throughout the 1970s, they remained a competent enough side but simply could not hold on to players long enough. Too many good players moved to other clubs but star winger Elgan Rees was a model of loyalty. While others left, Elgan stayed and scored try after try, and the most-heard call at The Gnoll was 'Give it to Elgan!' Eventually he was rewarded with his first Welsh cap at Murrayfield in a try-scoring debut in 1979, and played 13 times for Wales, scoring 6 tries, and also scored in a 'non-cap' game against the New Zealand Maoris. He went on two Lions tours in 1977 and 1980 as Neath's first 'double' Lion, captained the club to glory in the 1980s and later became chairman.

Above right: The Blacks suffered badly from player defections including Glyn Shaw, an outstandingly athletic prop from Seven Sisters. Shaw was cast in the mould of the great Neath forwards of the past and earned 12 caps for Wales, but found his path blocked by Pontypool's Charlie Faulkner. A confrontational scrummager, Shaw was ahead of his time and a real live wire in the loose who would surely have benefited from the speeding-up of the modern game. Glyn Shaw joined Widnes RL in November 1977 just as he was approaching his prime. He won rugby league international honours but Welsh rugby missed out on his best years.

Right, opposite above and opposite below: On 1 November 1972 Neath played what might be termed the first European Cup final. As Welsh Cup winners, the Blacks travelled to play Béziers, the French champions, in a special fixture to mark the opening of the Parc des Princes. Sadly, Neath travelled minus four of the front five who had done so much to lift the Cup and they could not match the Béziers pack. The French side led 13-10 at half time and ran out 29-17 winners.

RUGBY   ## HIER AU PARC DES PRINCES

BÉZIERS, en écrasant NEATH
devient une valeur internationale

A.S. BEZIERS b. NEATH, 29-17 (à la mi-temps, 13-10).

A.S. BEZIERS : 5 essais, Astre (3e), Navarro (12e), Paco (46e), Costantino (48), Cantoni (55e) ; 2 transformations, Astre, 1 transformation, 1 but, Cantoni (42e).

NEATH : 2 essais, Collier (30e), Poole (8e) ; 2 buts, Ball (10e, 60e) ; 1 but, Lauder (37e).

Parc des Princes, beau temps, bon terrain. Recette : 142.754,50 F pour 7.492 entrées payantes. Arbitre : D. Jones (Angleterre).

L'ARBITRE s'appelait M. Jones, comme Dai Jones, le personnage de l'imagerie populaire galloise. Si on l'avait dit aux spectateurs du Parc des Princes, ils auraient cru volontiers que ce brave Anglais, au lieu de débarquer de Nottingham, avait voyagé dans les fourgons de Neath, champion du Pays de Galles, et qu'il s'était juré de défendre sa cause. M. Jones fit ainsi son expérience des réactions d'un public très particulier. Il ne s'en est pas étonné. Car il est bien connu en Grande-Bretagne que nous sommes des gens impossibles. Notons cependant que l'on avait en apparence quelques raisons de manifester de la mauvaise humeur. Durant la première période de ce match qui opposait le club numéro 1 de Galles et le numéro 1 de France, nos compatriotes furent pénalisés quatre fois plus que leurs adversaires.

Et cela eut pour effet de retarder la marche de l'A.S. Béziers vers une victoire qu'elle a parfaitement méritée.

L'animateur de Neath, l'ancien international aux 42 capes, Rees Stephens, lui-même ancien combattant féroce, venu à grandes guides de Llanelli où il avait assisté la veille à la défaite des All Blacks, ne broncha pas en assistant à la déroute des siens, à peu près unique dans les annales de sa petite ville. Il associa dans un même éloge tous les avants français qui furent directement à l'origine d'un véritable exploit :

— *Certes, nous avions dû remanier notre propre « pack » en première et en deuxième ligne pour pallier certaines indisponibilités, mais nous ne pensions pas que les Biterrois fussent à la fois si forts et si bien organisés.*

L'A.S. Béziers est rassurée à propos de la valeur du style de jeu qu'elle a délibérément choisi depuis 1967 sous l'influence de son entraîneur Raoul Barrière, un style de jeu qui ne sacrifie pas l'essentiel aux effets de manchette. Les cinq essais des Languedociens furent inscrits par des éléments des lignes arrière, mais chacun prit sa source dans la mêlée fermée.

Cette seule phase valut aux visiteurs une inoubliable humiliation. Elle les laissa pratiquement sans ressources. Ils avaient en troisième ligne deux authentiques internationaux, un Gallois (Dai Morris) et un Ecossais (Bill Lauder) ; leur présence passa à peu près inaperçue alors qu'on garde encore l'image des charges d'Olivier Saisset (un troisième ligne), d'Alain Estève (un deuxième ligne) ou d'André Lubrano (le talonneur).

Dès la troisième minute, en suivant la progression de ses hommes bien soudés pour assurer la poussée la plus efficace, le demi Richard Astre sut que rien de grave ne pouvait arriver à l'équipe dont il est le capitaine. Sa mêlée lui avait permis déjà de franchir la frontière défendue par Neath. D'autres s'engageaient dans la même voie.

Jean Denis.

Above: The final season for Neath Grammar School was 1972/73. They had an unparalleled record of success, and their famous blue and gold ranks had produced so many senior All Blacks. The Welsh grammar school system gave way to 'comprehensive' education and many blame its passing for Welsh rugby's decline. Neath RFC paid tribute by hosting the school XV. PE master Ron Trimnell (who also coached Swansea and later joined the Neath committee) is pictured with some of his charges in their school blazers. Many played for Neath – Hywel Guy, Ian Hopkins, Tim Roberts, Jeff Herdman, Cuan O'Shea, Andrew Shufflebotham, David Lewis, Clive Hopkins, Robert Hughes, Bruce Bradley, Byron Bater and Wyn Ellis, while David Richards went on to play for Swansea, Wales and the Lions.

Right: In January 1973, Neath combined with Aberavon for the final time to take on a touring side and were thrashed 43-3 as the New Zealanders turned on arguably the best display of the tour.

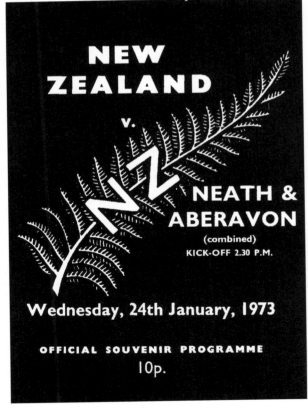

NEW ZEALAND

v.

NEATH & ABERAVON
(combined)
KICK-OFF 2.30 P.M.

Wednesday, 24th January, 1973

OFFICIAL SOUVENIR PROGRAMME
10p.

NEW ZEALAND

15	J. F. KARAM	. . . .	Full Back
14	D. A. HALES	. . . .	Right Wing
13	I. A. HURST	. . . .	Right Centre
12	M. SAYERS	. . . .	Left Centre
11	G. B. BATTY	. . . .	Left Wing
10	R. E. BURGESS	. . . .	Outside Half
9	G. L. COLLING	. . . .	Inside Half
1	G. J. WHITING	. . . .	Prop
2	R. W. NORTON	. . . .	Hooker
3	F. McNICHOL	. . . .	Prop
4	H. H. MACDONALD	. . . .	Lock
5	A. HADEN	. . . .	Lock
6	K. W. STEWART	. . . .	Flanker
8	A. J. WYLLIE	. . . .	No. 8
7	I. A. KIRKPATRICK	. . . .	Flanker

NEATH & ABERAVON
(COMBINED)
Colours: Red and Black hooped jerseys with white Maltese cross; white shorts

15	WYNNE DAVIES	. . . .	(N)	Full Back
14	DAVID JENKINS	. . . .	(N)	Right Wing
13	GLEN BALL (Capt.)	. . . .	(N)	Right Centre
12	JEFF THOMAS	. . . .	(A)	Left Centre
11	KEN COLLIER	. . . .	(N)	Left Wing
10	JOHN BEVAN	. . . .	(A)	Outside Half
9	CLIVE SHELL	. . . .	(A)	Inside Half
1	GLYN SHAW*	. . . .	(N)	Prop
2	MORTON HOWELLS (Vice Capt.)	.	(A)	Hooker
3	ROY LEWIS	. . . .	(N)	Prop
4	ALAN MARTIN	. . . .	(A)	Lock
5	BILLY MAINWARING*	. . . . .	(A)	Lock
6	DAVID MORRIS*	. . . .	(N)	Flanker
8	WILSON LAUDER*	. . . . . .	(N)	No. 8
7	OGWEN ALEXANDER	. . . . .	(A)	Flanker

* indicates international
Reserves:- John Poole, David Parker, Martin Davies, Norman Rees, Stuart Hodgson. (all Neath)

Touch Judge: Mr. C. THOMAS (Cardiff   Referee: Mr. P. E. HUGHES (Burnley)   Touch Judge: Mr. T. R. R. BEBB (Swansea)

Music by the Band of the Welsh Guards
Director of Music Major Desmond Walker, A.R.C.M.
by kind permission of the Lt. Col. Commanding the Regt. Col. J. W. T. A. Malcolm

The match programme lists John Bevan at outside half but he pulled out on the morning of the match and his place was taken by Dai Parker. Bevan, a Neath Grammar School product, originally played for Neath and captained Neath Cricket Club for many seasons. After transferring his rugby allegiance to Aberavon, he was capped by Wales in 1974 and later coached the national team before his untimely death at a tragically young age.

WEST WALES

Full Back	15	WYNNE DAVIES (Neath)
Right Wing	14	ANDY HILL (Llanelli)
Right Centre	13	RAY GRAVELLE (Llanelli)
Left Centre	12	DAVID JENKINS (Neath)
Left Wing	11	VIVIAN JENKINS (Bridgend)
Outside Half	10	IAN LEWIS (Bridgend)
Inside Half	9	CLIVE SHELL (Aberavon) (Captain)
Prop	1	CHRIS CHARLES (Llanelli)
Hooker	2	ROY THOMAS (Llanelli)
Prop	3	WALTER WILLIAMS (Neath)
Lock	4	BARRIE DAVIES (Neath)
Lock	5	STUART HODGSON (Neath)
Wing Forward	6	GARETH JENKINS (Llanelli)
No. 8	8	HEFIN JENKINS (Llanelli)
Wing Forward	7	OGWYN ALEXANDER (Aberavon)

Replacements:—16—Lyndon Thomas (Bridgend); 17—John Bevan (Aberavon); 18—Selwyn Williams (Llanelli); 19—Morton Howells (Aberavon); 20—Billy Howe (Maesteg); 21—Mike Griffiths (Llanelli).

AUSTRALIA

Full Back	25	ARTHUR NEIL McGILL (Drummoyne Club, Sydney)	5'9½"	172lbs.
Right Wing	20	DAVID RONALD BURNET (Gordon Club, Sydney)	5'11½"	187lbs.
Right Centre	21	REX DAVID L'ESTRANGE (Brothers Club, Brisbane)	5'9"	172lbs.
Left Centre	18	GEOFFREY ARNOLD SHAW (Kiama)	5'10"	196lbs.
Left Wing	23	JEFFREY JAMES McLEAN (Teachers Club, Brisbane)	6'0"	190lbs.
Outside Half	19	PETER GEORGE ROWLES (Wollongong Country)	5'8"	168lbs.
Inside Half	15	RODNEY GRAHAM HAUSER (South Australia)	5'6½"	154lbs.
Prop Forward	3	RONALD GRAHAM (St. George Club, Sydney)	6'1"	218lbs.
Hooker	1	CHRIS. MICHAEL CARBERRY (Sydney II)	5'11"	182lbs.
Prop Forward	5	STUART GRANT MACDOUGALL (Western Districts, Canberra)	6'1"	210lbs.
2nd Row	7	REGINALD ALAN SMITH (Northern Suburbs, Sydney)	6'4"	231lbs.
2nd Row	8	STUART CARLTON GREGORY (Eastwood Club, Sydney)	6'4"	224lbs.
Wing Forward	13	BRUCE BATTISHALL (Sydney) (Late replacement for C. Cornelson)		
No. 8	12	KENNETH GEORGE McCURRACH (Eastwood Club, Sydney)	5'1"	214lbs.
Wing Forward	11	PETER DAVID SULLIVAN (Captain) (Gordon Club, Sydney)	6'2"	200lbs.

Replacements:—14—John Hipwell (Newcastle); 17—Geoffrey Richardson (Brothers Club, Brisbane); 24 Russell Fairfax (Randwick, Sydney); 2—Michael Freney (Brothers Club, Brisbane); 4—John Howard (Sydney University); 10—Richard Cocks (Brothers Club, Brisbane)

Referee: J. R. West (Ireland)   Touch Judges: Ron Lewis (Llangynwyd); W. J. O. Morse (Tenby)

On 6 November 1973, West Wales lost to Australia at Aberavon with five Neath men included.

Tough prop Walter Williams won his Welsh cap against France in 1974. The Neath Athletic graduate, who farmed near Resolven, made his debut in 1965 and appeared up until 1977. Never beaten, he set the trend for future farming front rows and his early death was tragic.

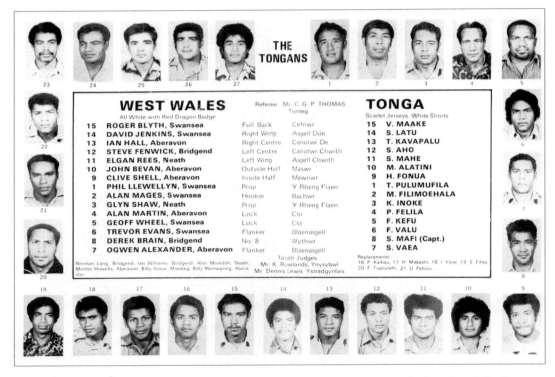

THE TONGANS

23 24 25 26 27 1 2 3 4 5

22

21

20

19 18 17 16 15 14 13 12 11 10 9

6

7

8

WEST WALES			Referee: Mr C. G. P. THOMAS. Tonteg	TONGA	
All White with Red Dragon Badge				Scarlet Jerseys, White Shorts	
15	ROGER BLYTH, Swansea	Full Back	Cefnwr	15	V. MAAKE
14	DAVID JENKINS, Swansea	Right Wing	Asgell Dde	14	S. LATU
13	IAN HALL, Aberavon	Right Centre	Canolwr De	13	T. KAVAPALU
12	STEVE FENWICK, Bridgend	Left Centre	Canolwr Chwith	12	S. AHO
11	ELGAN REES, Neath	Left Wing	Asgell Chwith	11	S. MAHE
10	JOHN BEVAN, Aberavon	Outside Half	Maswr	10	M. ALATINI
9	CLIVE SHELL, Aberavon	Inside Half	Mewnwr	9	H. FONUA
1	PHIL LLEWELLYN, Swansea	Prop	Y Rheng Flaen	1	T. PULUMUFILA
2	ALAN MAGES, Swansea	Hooker	Bachwr	2	M. FILIMOEHALA
3	GLYN SHAW, Neath	Prop	Y Rheng Flaen	3	K. INOKE
4	ALAN MARTIN, Aberavon	Lock	Clo	4	P. FELILA
5	GEOFF WHEEL, Swansea	Lock	Clo	5	F. KEFU
6	TREVOR EVANS, Swansea	Flanker	Blaenasgell	6	F. VALU
8	DEREK BRAIN, Bridgend	No. 8	Wythwr	8	S. MAFI (Capt.)
7	OGWEN ALEXANDER, Aberavon	Flanker	Blaenasgell	7	S. VAEA

Touch Judges

Norman Lang, Bridgend; Ian Williams, Bridgend; Alan Meredith, Neath; Morton Howells, Aberavon; Billy Howe, Maesteg; Billy Mainwaring, Aberavon.

Mr. K. Rowlands, Ynysybwl
Mr. Dennis Lewis, Ystradgynlais

Replacements
16. P. Kaihau, 17. H. Makaohi, 18. I. Vave, 19. S. Fifita, 20. F. Tupoulahi, 21. U. Pahulu.

Wales had its first glimpse of the Tongans in 1974, and Neath's Elgan Rees and Glyn Shaw helped West Wales overcome the tourists at Swansea on 12 October. A third Neath man, Alan Meredith, was on the replacements bench. Alan (son of former Neath captain D.T.) later joined Swansea and became a committeeman with the St Helen's club.

Neath's first captain was a Scottish international,
Dr T.P. Whittington, who led the club in 1871/72. The
Blacks had a second Scottish leader in 1974/75 and
1975/76 in back-row forward Wilson Lauder, who had
joined Neath in 1967 from Llantwit Major as a protégé of
Grahame Hodgson. A left-footed place-kicker, he soon
made his mark and was first capped in 1968 for Scotland
against Ireland in 1967 and toured both Argentina and
Australia on his way to 18 caps. After leaving Neath, he
finished his career at Maesteg.

Under the management of secretary Allan Benjamin, Neath embarked upon their most exotic trip
ever when they toured the West Indies in 1975, winning all six games and scoring 288 points in
the process. Here the team's biggest man, Robert Hughes, looks as if he is about to 'walk the
plank' on one of the many sightseeing expeditions enjoyed by the side. The All Blacks defeated the
Jamaica RFU President's XV (90-6), Privateers (31-3), Montego Bay (22-3) and the Jaa-Baas
41-21, before crossing to Grand Cayman where they beat the Island XV 52-3 and racked up a
similar scoreline against the Grand Cayman Select XV. Outside half Peter Davies (like his brother
Wynne from the Crynant club) scored 48 points and three-quarter Mike Jenkins (a Neath Athletic
product) scored 14 tries. 'Lavish hospitality and a wonderful experience,' summed up
Allan Benjamin.

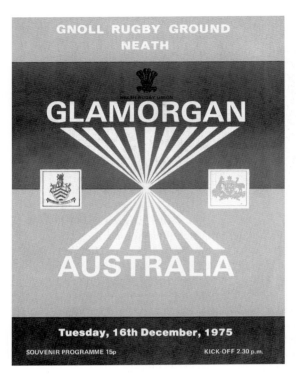

The Gnoll hosted the Glamorgan County v. Australia match on 16 December 1975. There was little for the home fans to cheer, though, as the tourists ran out comfortable winners. Robert Hughes and Wilson Lauder represented Neath, with Martyn Davies and hooker Mike Richards on the bench. Grahame Hodgson coached the county side who really needed more training sessions together.

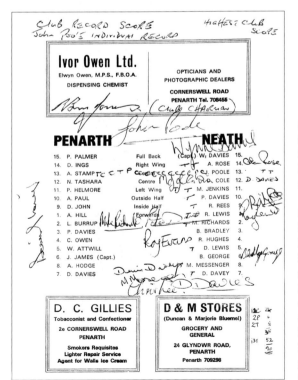

Left: The match programme from the game when centre John Poole broke the individual points record when he scored 38 points in the 90-10 win over Penarth on 20 April 1977.

Opposite below: On 15 March 1977, a benefit match was played between the Neath 1971/72 cup-winners side and the local Metal Box RFC (since defunct) in memory of their late hooker David Elias. Brian Thomas frequently brought the cup winners together for charity and exhibition matches, although for this game it was necessary to make one change. David Jenkins had 'gone north' so his place was taken by Neath's rising young winger Elgan Rees.

Above: 'You gave us some glorious rugby'. That was the verdict of Wally Thomas of the *Neath Guardian*, who had covered Neath for over forty years from the end of the Second World War. The 1976/77 season was Neath's best since the centenary season five years earlier. The Blacks' record read: Played 44, Won 29, Drawn 3, Lost 12, Points For 987 (beat the record of 930 set by the championship-winning side of 1928/29), Points Against 512. Treherbert-product Poole scored 269 points (14 tries, 57 conversions, 32 penalties and 1 dropped goal) to beat the previous record of 261 points, again set in 1928/29 by another centre, Emrys Jones, who scored 7 tries, 83 conversions, 18 penalties and 5 dropped goals). Poole's ex-Treherbert team-mate Alan Rose bagged 27 tries, but both were to leave Neath for Pontypridd. From left to right, back row: H.M. Powell, W. Thomas, H. Mort, B. Dennis, J. Prichard, J. James, B. Allen, E. Case, R. Parker (all Committee). Standing: N. Biggs (Assistant Secretary), Martin Richards (Physio), S. Davies, C. Niven, T. Dennis, M. Messenger, R. Evans, R. Hughes, G. Shaw, S. Williams, W. Lauder, M. Arnall. H.E. Rees, D. Davey, Mike Richards, D. Lewis, T.O. Jones. Seated: R. Rees, A. Rose, P. Davies, R. Thomas (Treasurer), J. Poole, R.B. Jones (Chairman), W. Davies (Captain), A. Benjamin (Secretary), D. Davies, R. Davies (Fixture Secretary), D. Cole, M. Jenkins. Front: R. Lewis, M. Thomas (Coach), P. Morgan, M. Davies (Player/Coach).

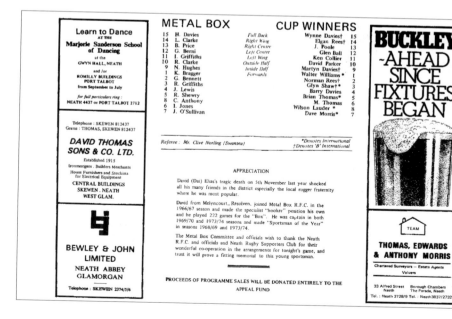

LLANELLI

Todays Match Ball Presented by ALCAN METAL CENTRES

15	KERI COSLETT	Cefnwr	Full Back
14	ANDY HILL	Asgell Dde	Right Wing
13	ROY BERGIERS	Canolwr Dde	Right Centre
12	RAY GRAVELL		
11	DAVID NICHOLAS		
10	PHIL BENNETT	Maswr	Outside Half
9	SELWYN WILLIAMS	Mewnwr	
1	CHARLES THOMAS	Y Rhedd	Prop
2	CHRIS DAVIES		
3	JOHN WILLIAMS		
4	ROGER POWELL	Clo	Lock
5	PHIL MAY	Clo	Lock
6	STEVE THOMAS	Blaenasgell	Flanker
8	HEFIN JENKINS	Wythwr	No 8
7	KEITH WILLIAMS	Blaenasgell	Flanker

Referee : Mr. D. M. DAVIES, Penclawdd

Royal Regt. of Wales

15	J. DAVIES	1st. Btn.
14	B. REYNOLDS	Army & Comb. Serv
13	S. JACKSON	Army & Comb. Serv
12	W. DAVIES	4th (V) Btn.
11	M. CHINNOCK	1st Btn
10	K. REES (Capt.)	Depot Crickhowell
9	M. DAVIES	4th (V) Btn.
1	M. MILLS	4th (V) Btn.
2	T. WEST	Depot Crickhowell
3	P. LANGFORD	4th (V) Btn.
4	B. DAVIES	4th (V) Btn.
5	S. FLOWER	3rd Btn
6	D. DAVEY	4th (V) Btn.
8	W. LAUDER	Guest Player
7	P. BEARD	3rd Btn.

Replacement — N. Pearce, Powys ACF

On 24 September 1977, five Neath players turned out for the Royal Regiment of Wales against Llanelli. The Territorial Army connections of prop Phil Langford afforded 'recruits' Martyn Davies, Barrie Davies, Wilson Lauder and Dennis Davey the opportunity to meet the Prince of Wales beforehand.

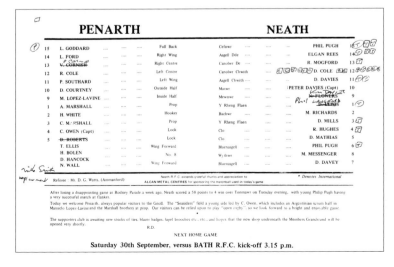

PENARTH			NEATH	
15	L. GODDARD	Full Back	Cefnwr	PHIL PUGH	16
14	L. FORD	Right Wing	Asgell Dde	ELGAN REES	14
13	V. CORNISH	Right Centre	Canolwr De	R. MOGFORD	13
12	R. COLE	Left Centre	Canolwr Mewn	D. COLE	12
11	P. SOUTHARD	Left Wing	Asgell Chwith	D. DAVIES	11
10	D. COURTNEY	Outside Half	Maswr	PETER DAVIES (Capt)	10
9	M. LOPEZ-LAVINE	Inside Half	Mewnwr	S. FLOWERS	9
1	A. MARSHALL	Prop	Y Rheng Flaen	M. RICHARDS	2
2	H. WHITE	Hooker	Bachwr	D. MILLS	3
3	C. MARSHALL	Prop	Y Rheng Flaen	R. HUGHES	4
4	C. OWEN (Capt)	Lock	Clo	D. MATHIAS	5
5	D. ROBERTS	Lock	Clo	PHIL PUGH	6
	T. ELLIS	Wing Forward	Blaenasgell	M. MESSENGER	8
	H. BOLEN	No. 8	Wythwr	D. DAVEY	7
	D. HANCOCK				
	N. WALL	Wing Forward	Blaenasgell		

Referee : Mr. D. G. Watts (Ammanford)

Neath R.F.C. extends grateful thanks and appreciation to
ALCAN METAL CENTRES for sponsoring the matchball used in today's game

* Denotes International

After losing a disappointing game at Rodney Parade a week ago, Neath scored a 58 points to 4 win over Tonmawr on Tuesday evening, with young Philip Pugh having a very successful match at flanker.

Today we welcome Penarth, always popular visitors to the Gnoll. The "Seasiders" field a young side led by C. Owen, which includes an Argentinian scrum half in Manuelo Lopez-Lavine and the Marshall brothers at prop. Our visitors can be relied upon to play "open rugby", so we look forward to a bright and enjoyable game.

The supporters club is awaiting new stocks of ties, blazer badges, lapel brooches etc., etc. and hopes that the new shop underneath the Members Grandstand will be opened very shortly.

R.D.

NEXT HOME GAME

Saturday 30th September, versus BATH R.F.C. kick-off 3.15 p.m.

Neath enjoyed an 83-3 win over Penarth on 23 September 1978, centre David Cole from Gorseinon scoring 31 points through 2 tries, 10 conversions and a penalty. Playing opposite him for Penarth was namesake Robert, who is now a leading Welsh rugby writer with the Westgate Agency in Cardiff.

Programme published by Swansea Rugby Supporters Club.
Secretary : Mr. Arthur Davies, 27 Queens Rd , Sketty, Swansea

Derek Quinnell,
Captain

Referee: Mr. A. W. WELSBY (England)

Graham Mourie,
Captain

WEST WALES XV   NEW ZEALAND

West Wales XV		Position		New Zealand
15	R. W. BLYTH (Swansea) †	Cefnwr	Full Back	15 B. J. McKECHNIE (Southland)
14	E. REES (Neath)	Asgell Dde	Right Wing	14 B. G. WILLIAMS (Auckland)
13	R. W. R. GRAVELL (Llanelli) †	Canolwr De	Right Centre	13 W. M. OSBORNE (Wanganui)
12	R. T. E. BERGIERS (Llanelli) †	Canolwr Chwith	Left Centre	12 J. L. JAFFRAY (Otago)
11	J. J. WILLIAMS (Llanelli) †	Asgell Chwith	Left Wing	11 S. S. WILSON (Wellington)
10	D. S. RICHARDS (Swansea)	Maswr	Outside Half	10 O. D. BRUCE (Canterbury)
9	C. SHELL (Aberavon) †	Mewnwr	Inside Half	9 M. W. DONALDSON (Manawatu)
1	J. RICHARDSON (Aberavon) †	Y Rheng Flaen	Prop	1 B. R. JOHNSTONE (Auckland)
2	J. HERDMAN (Swansea)	Bachwr	Hooker	2 J. E. BLACK (Canterbury)
3	P. D. LLEWELLYN (Swansea)	Y Rheng Flaen	Prop	3 G. A. KNIGHT (Manawatu)
4	A. J. MARTIN (Aberavon) †	Clo	Lock	4 F. J. OLIVER (Otago) / J. K. FLEMING (Wellington)
5	G. A. D. WHEEL (Swansea) †	Clo	Lock	5 A. M. HADEN (Auckland)
6	G. ROBERTS (Swansea)	Blaenasgell	Flanker	6 G. N. MOURIE (Capt.) (Taranaki)
8	D. L. QUINNELL (Capt.) (Llanelli) †	Wythwr	No. 8	8 G. E. SEEAR (Otago)
7	T. P. EVANS (Swansea) †	Blaenasgell	Flanker	7 W. G. GRAHAM (Otago)

Replacements		Replacements:
Peter Morgan (Llanelli)	Richard Moriarty (Swansea)	Clive Currie (Canterbury) Billy Bush (Canterbury)
Selwyn Williams (Llanelli)	Alan Davies (South Wales Police)	Eddie Dunn (North Auckland) Andy Dalton (Counties)
Billy James (Aberavon)	† Denotes International	David Loveridge (Taranaki) Leicester Rutledge (Southland)

Elgan Rees was Neath's only representative in the West Wales side that crashed to New Zealand at St Helen's on 25 October 1978.

HAAGSCHE   NEATH

No.	Haagsche	Position	Welsh	Neath	No.
15	A. NEDERLOF *B	Full Back	Cefnwr	K. ROBERTS	15
14	P. SPEIJK *	Right Wing	Asgell Dde	D. DAVIES	14
13	H van DAM *	Right Centre	Canolwr De	P. WOODLAND	13
12	J. DINGELMANS	Left Centre	Canolwr Chwith	D. COLE / STEVEN BENNETT	12
11	P. BARNEVELD	Left Wing	Asgell Chwith	B. TAYLOR	11
10	T. OOSTWIJN *	Outside Half	Maswr	PETER DAVIES (Capt)	10
9	V. TRIEBERT *(Capt)	Inside Half	Mewnwr	C. GNOJEK	9
1	M. RUITERMAN	Prop	Y Rheng Flaen	A. JONES	1
2	J. SCHAAP *	Hooker	Bachwr	P. HITCHINS	2
3	T. van der LOOS *	Prop	Y Rheng Flaen	R. RATTI	3
4	T. DORST *	Lock	Clo	R. HUGHES	4
5	P. ENGELHART *B	Lock	Clo	S. DANDO	5
6	G. DONGELMANS	Wing Forward	Blaenasgell	P. PUGH	6
8	R. RIJKE	No. 8	Wythwr	H. GRIFFITHS	8
7	W. van der LOOS	Wing Forward	Blaenasgell	P. JONES	7

Replacements : R. Mogford : M. Richards

Mr. Alun Richards (Caldicot)

Neath R.F.C. extends grateful thanks and appreciation to
ALCAN METAL CENTRES for sponsoring the matchball used in today's game

* Denotes International

Next Home Game
Tuesday next 20th March v. N.Z. "CANTABRIANS
Kick-off 6.30 p.m.
Tickets on sale after tonight's match

Neath's overseas links continued in March 1979 with the visit of teams from Holland and New Zealand. Haagsche were beaten 36-0.

CANTABRIANS N.Z.   NEATH

15	W. F. McCORMIC *	....	....	....	Full Back	Cefnwr	....	....	J. PRITCHARD	15
14	B. FRASER		....	....	Right Wing	Asgell Dde	....	....	ELGAN REES *	14
13	K. J. KEANE	....		....	Right Centre	Canolwr De	....	....	D. COLE	13
12	J. E. MORGAN *	....		....	Left Centre	Canolwr Chwith		....	R. MOGFORD	12
11	A. JEFFERD	....			Left Wing	Asgell Chwith	....	....	B. TAYLOR	11
10	D. J. ROBERTSON *	....			Outside Half	Maswr	....	....	PETER DAVIES (Capt)	10
9	L. J. DAVIS *	....		....	Inside Half	Mewnwr	....		N. FLOWERS	9
1	B. THOMPSON	....			Prop	Y Rheng Flaen		....	D. LEWIS	1
2	TANE NORTON *	....		....	Hooker	Bachwr	....		M. RICHARDS	2
3	K. J. TANNER *	....		....	Prop	Y Rheng Flaen		....	D. MILLS	3
4	H. H. MacDONALD *	....			Lock	Clo	....		R. HUGHES	4
5	V. E. T. STEWART			....	Lock	Clo	....		S. DANDO	5
6	K. J. STEWART *	....		....	Wing Forward	Blaenasgell	....		M. MESSENGER	6
8	ALEX WYLLIE *	....	....	....	No. 8	Wythwr	....		PHIL PUGH	8
7	D. THOMPSON	....	....	....	Wing Forward	Blaenasgell	....		P. JONES	7

Replacements   K. ROBERTS   P. HITCHINS

Referee : Mr. Winstone Jones (Ammanford)

Neath R.F.C. extends grateful thanks and appreciation to
ALCAN METAL CENTRES for sponsoring the matchball used in today's game

* Denotes International

The Cantabrians (including eleven All Blacks) edged a win before a huge crowd.

Neath RFC 1978/79, skippered by Peter Davies, won 22, drew 3 and lost 19 of their 44 games, scoring 704 points with 522 against. Centre David Cole scored 140 points including 12 tries. From left to right, back row: H.M. Powell, R. Williams, K. Davies, W. Thomas, R. Parker, E. Case, J. James, D. Bennett, R. Trimnell, E.R. John (all Committee). Standing: T.O. Jones (Committee), R. John, A. Omar (Physio), P.M. Jones, C. Jones, D. Mills, R. Hughes, P. Rawlins, J. Rawlins, R. Ratti, P. Pugh, C. Haste, M. Thomas (Team Secretary), N. Biggs (Committee), M. Davies (Coach). Seated: R. Brooks (Ballboy), S. Davies (Committee), K. Roberts, B. Taylor, A. Benjamin (Secretary), P. Davies (Captain), R.B. Jones (Chairman), M. Richards, J. Prichard (Treasurer), D. Cole, R. Davies (Fixture Secretary), C. Gnojek.

Neath RFC, 1979/80. This photograph was rather obviously taken on the same day as the 1978/79 version with minor placing adjustments. Neath won 26, drew 3 and lost 19 of 48 fixtures, scoring 780 points with 661 against. Full-back John Pritchard, a goal-kicking drayman from Ynysybwl, scored 193 points. Able to kick with both feet with equal facility, Pritchard previously played for Cardiff and he is remembered for a virtuoso effort that inspired Neath to a win at Llanelli, where he landed 6 goals for an epic 18-17 victory. From left to right, back row: H.M. Powell, R. Williams, K. Davies, W. Thomas, G. Williams, R. Parker, E. Case, J. James, D. Bennett, N. Biggs, E.R. John (all Committee). Standing: M. Thomas (Team Secretary), R. John, T.O. Jones (Committee), B. Taylor, A. Omar (Physio), P. Jones, C. Jones, D. Mills, R. Hughes, P. Rawlins, J. Rawlins, R. Ratti, P. Pugh, C. Haste, R.J. Trimnell (Committee). Seated: R. Brooks (Ballboy), S. Davies (Committee), M. Richards, K. Roberts, A. Benjamin (Secretary), D. Cole (Captain), R.B. Jones (Chairman), C. Gnojek, J. Prichard (Treasurer), P. Davies, R. Davies (Fixture Secretary), M. Davies (Coach).

In 1980/81, the Welsh Rugby Union celebrated its centenary (nine years after Neath!) and Neath's contribution, as the Principality's oldest senior club, was to host the Wales v. France 'B'-international.

The Post Office Centenary Match

WALES 'B'
V.
FRANCE 'B'

CYMRU 'B'
V.
FFRAINC 'B'

Gnoll Ground, Neath
Saturday 11th October, 1980
OFFICIAL PROGRAMME 20p

Neath RFC 1981/82, led by hooker Mike Richards, won 28, drew 1 and lost 18 of 47 games with another Athletic product Alan Edmunds scoring 17 tries in his first season out of youth rugby. Including the Canada tour, Neath scored 786 points with utility back Phil Jones scoring 151 of them. From left to right, back row: K. Davies, J. James, G. Williams, B. Davies, D. Bennett, W. Thomas, B. Allen, R. Parker (all Committee). Standing: N. Biggs (Committee), C. Niven (Committee), J. Hopkins, S. Dando, A. Vaughan, P. Rawlins, C. Jones, G. Jones, P. Bogdan, N. Mannion, R.J. Trimnell (Committee). Seated: H.M. Powell (Committee), H.E. Rees, J. Prichard (Treasurer), D. Randall, R.B. Jones (Chairman), M. Richards (Captain), A. Benjamin (Secretary), D. Davies, R. Davies (Fixture Secretary), M. Davies (Coach), S. Davies (Committee). Front: C. Gnojek, S. Powell, A. Edmunds, C. Thomas.

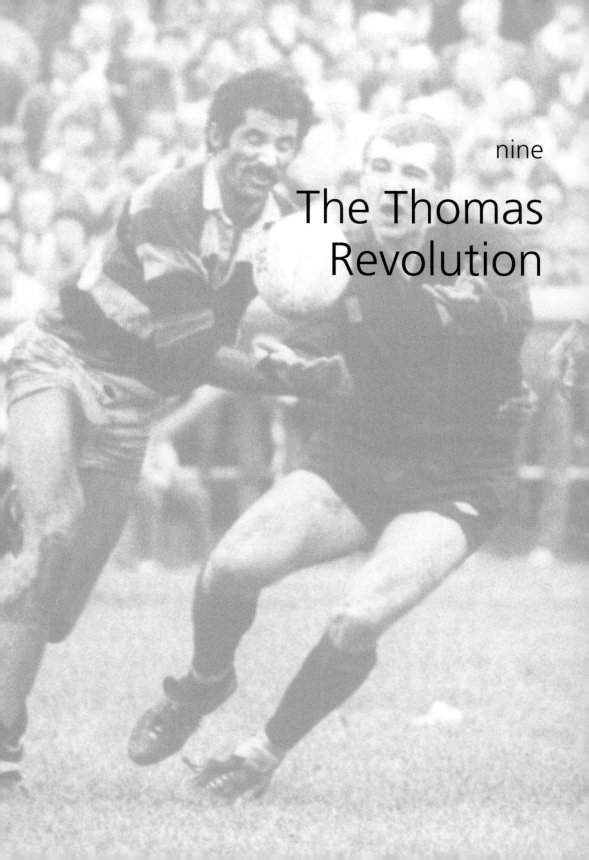

nine

The Thomas Revolution

During his playing years, Brian Thomas brought a real hard edge to Neath's play. Like all the great Neath forwards he would simply not accept second best and would never tolerate lack of effort. A metallurgist in the steel industry, Thomas applied his management skills to Neath RFC when he rejoined the Neath committee in 1982/83. Aided by a solid group of henchmen, many of them team-mates from his playing days, he got Neath back on track. Brian (pictured centre in a steamy training-night dressing room), his coaches Ron Waldron (left) and Glen Ball (right), together with fitness expert Alan Roper and team secretary David Shaw laid the plans for Neath's re-emergence, and the club embarked upon a decade of real achievement that brought packed houses to The Gnoll to see Neath take on the world's best.

BAYONNE		NEATH
15 E. OTAZO ^M	Full Back	C. Bridgewater 15
14 D. Curutchat _J	Right Wing	* H. E. Rees (Capt.) 14
13 P. Perrier	Right Centre	D. Jacob 13
12 P. Peytavin 'B'	Left Centre	C. Jones 12
11 D. Urruty	Left Wing	S. Powell 11
10 P. Alvarez ^M	Outside Half	I. Davies 10
9 P. Pucheu _J	Inside Half	G. Jones 9
1 J-M. Ithurbide	Prop.	S. Dando 1
2 Y. Cedarry	Hooker	M. Richards 2
3 J. Garat 'B'	Prop.	D. Mills 3
4 J-L. Fabre _J	Lock	R. Hughes 4
5 A. Gastambide	Lock	A. N. Other 5
6 R. Navarron	Wing Forward	L. Jones 6
8 A. Fabre _J	No. 8	D. Morgan 8
7 C. Cabanes	Wing Forward	C. Jones 7

Subs :

Subs : C. Gnojek, P. Langford

* denotes International   'B' denotes B 'Cap'   M denotes Military 'Cap'   J denotes Junior International

SPONSOR
The Club would like to express sincere thanks and appreciation to PARKHURST & CO., NEATH who have sponsored the BALL in this evenings match.

Next Home Games - Neath v. Newport Saturday, 17th September, kick off 3 p.m.
Saturday, 10th September, Neath Youth v. Glynneath

A key part of the Thomas plan was to harden-up Neath by exposure to French sides – 'the best available to us in Europe.' As such, Neath hosted and beat Bayonne on Monday 5 September 1983.

The concept of 'team management' was to bring Neath out of the dark ages and lift them to the heady heights of rugby achievement. Many star players would make it big in the next decade but the roots of the Thomas revolution were based firmly on a core of solid, largely unheralded Neath men, like Steve Powell, Carl Gnojek, Phil Langford, Steve Dando, Dai Morgan and Gareth Jones. Among them was hooker Mike Richards, good enough to sit on the replacements bench for Wales a record 21 times but never capped. In an era when caps are almost given away it is hard to believe that nobody left the field. But Mike would not have wanted it any other way. He joined Neath in 1972/73 and came out of semi-retirement with Neath Athletic 2nds to avert a hooking crisis in 1998/99, giving him easily the lengthiest career span in the history of the club.

Pontypool's international flanker Mark Brown challenges Neath's dynamic open-side flanker Lyn Jones, a Welsh Youth cap, who joined Neath from Cwmafan at the start of the 1983/84 season. His quick-thinking and speed soon added a new dimension to Neath's expansive style of play. He briefly played for Llanelli, helping them win both League and cup, before returning to The Gnoll as coach. Briefly in charge at Treorchy, he was an innovative coach of Neath during the professional era before becoming the first regional coach with Neath-Swansea Ospreys.

WELSH RUGBY UNION

NEATH v. JAPAN

THE GNOLL . NEATH

SATURDAY, 15th OCTOBER, 1983

kick off 3 p.m.

GROUND . . £2

Ray Williams

Secretary WRU

N⁰ 8517

THE AKAI MATCH

Gnoll Ground, Neath
Saturday, 15th October, 1983
Kick off 3 p.m.

NEATH

JAPAN

OFFICIAL PROGRAMME - 40p

Above and left: The ticket and programme for the Neath *v.* Japan game at The Gnoll, 15 October 1983. The match was drawn.

The Schweppes Cup final, 28 April 1984 – a wine-bottle label containing the two teams and the score.

Neath RFC, 1983/84 – the team that put Neath back on the map. From left to right, back row: S. Powell, B. Williams, K. Jones, D.G. Jones, P. Pugh, J. Willis, C. Jones, A. Vaughan, D. Jacob. Standing: P. Langford, G. Tucker, P. Hitchings, D. Morgan, S. Dando, A. Hopkins, R. Hughes, H. Richards, T. Waldron, J. Diamond (Trainer). Seated: K. Hollifield, C. Bridgewater, N. Harris, B. Childs, H.E. Rees (Captain), M. Richards, G.L. Jones, L. Jones, I. Davies, C. Gnojek.

NEATH RUGBY FOOTBALL CLUB

✠

SEASON 1983-84

PLAYED 52 ;   WON 31 ;   DRAWN 2 ;   LOST 19.
POINTS FOR 846 ;   POINTS AGAINST 690.

Player	Appear-ances	Tries	Conver-sions	Penalties	Drop Goals	Totals	Appearances 1969-70 to 1983-84
C. Bridgewater	34	7				28	34
K. Bowen	1						1
R. Bevan	1		1	2		8	1
M. Bannister	1						1
B. Childs	25	1	10	3	5	48	26
R. Carhart	1						1
I. Davies	9		4	4		20	32
S. Dando	38	1				4	208
A. Davies	2	1		1		7	2
S. Davies	2						2
J. Davies	9	1		2	2	16	15
N. Davies	1				1	3	1
P. Evans	2				1	3	2
J. Fear	5		1	2		8	5
S. Foster	2						2
D. Glover	14	5				20	18
C. Gnojek	19	5				20	152
J. Griffiths	1						1
K. Hollyfied	8						8
R. Hughes	21	2				8	300
A. Hopkins	30	3				12	30
N. Harris	35	5	49	60	1	301	77 = 29⁹
P. Hitchins	21						58
K. Jones	39	7				28	50
I. Jeffries	2	1				4	2
G. Jones	29	7				28	29
G. Jones	19	2				8	99
D. Jacobs	35	15				60	67
L. Jones	42	12				48	42
S. Jones	7	2		4		20	8
H. Jones	1						1
A. Jenkins	3						3
P. Langford	38	1				4	210
N. Llewellyn	1						1
S. Lewis	1						1
A. Lane	1						1
D. Mills	10						134
D. Morgan	31	2				8	61
R. Macallister	1						1
N. Mabadd	1						1
S. Oag	3	1				4	3
L. O'Conner	1						1
S. Powell	41	5				20	132
P. Pugh	18	1				4	62
A. Payne	2						2
S. Preedy	1						1
M. Richards	35	4				16	333
E. Rees (C)	26	14				56	212
M. Rowlands	3	1				4	3
H. Richards	19	1				4	19
H. Rees	1						1
D. Randall	4						68
R. Subbiani	1						1
G. Tucker	9	3				12	9
A. Vaughan	17						49
T. Waldron	4						37
D. Williams	3						5
B. Williams	22	3				12	22
G. Williams	4						4
J. Willis	21						30
K. Yates	1						1
TOTALS		113	65	78	10	846	
POINTS		452	130	234	30	846	

Including Cup Matches, Cup Final and Missionary Games.

Left: The official statistics for the 1983/84 season, when the 'Thomas Revolution' began to manifest itself with that cup-final appearance.

Above: When record points-scoring full-back Neale Harris (301 in 1983/84) joined South Wales Police, Neath found a ready-made replacement in Swansea University student Paul Thorburn, who had impressed the previous season when playing outside half for Ebbw Vale against the Blacks. Thorburn soon established himself as an even more prolific kicker than Harris, and shattered the club record by scoring 436 points. He earned 37 caps for Wales, captaining the national side on 10 occasions, and scored a then-record 304 points for his country. He made over 300 appearances for Neath, scored over 2,500 points and is credited with the longest goal kick in international rugby with his 70 yards 8½ inches penalty against Scotland in 1986.

No hiding place! Brian Thomas sought and found a certain type of forward: rough, rugged and ruthless – on the field anyway! Here, London Welsh's Clive Rees has attracted the attentions of three of the best (from left to right), Dai Morgan, Brian Williams and Mike Richards. Who'd want to be on the receiving end of that trio?

More action from the same game. Ron Waldron's work with the Welsh Youth brought a host of promising youngsters to The Gnoll. On the floor is Lyn Jones (later to coach the club), ready to receive is scrum-half Gareth Jones, who won the Lloyd Lewis award in the 1984 WRU Cup final, and shading his eyes is Jonathan Davies.

Above: Elgan Rees again skippered Neath RFC in 1984/85.

Left: A slightly nervous young outside half from Trimsaran made his bow for Neath in 1982/83. Unfortunately, a knee operation kept Jonathan Davies out of action for over a year until February 1984 when he tested it for Neath Athletic 2nds against Waunarlwydd 2nds in an international morning fixture at Court Herbert. A week later, he inspired Neath to a Schweppes Cup quarter-final win over Newport at The Gnoll and the rest, as they say, is history. Jonathan Davies captained the club that gave him his big opportunity in 1985/86 and 1986/87 before joining Llanelli and then Widnes RL. He enjoyed a brilliant career in both codes but many feel that Neath saw the best of him as an unfettered and unknown player. Tries against Bridgend and Bath will forever live in the memory and Jonathan went on to become one of Wales' all-time greats.

When Bath came to The Gnoll on 29 November 1986 the unofficial title of 'British champions' was at stake. Neath led the *Western Mail* championship and the Whitbread Merit Table, Bath led the John Smith's Merit Table, but a Jonathan Davies special spearheaded Neath's 26-9 win that took them to the top of the *Daily Telegraph* Anglo-Welsh table.

Neath RFC won the Whitbread Merit Table in 1986/87. Here, the championship flag is handed over by representatives of Whitbread to Neath chairman Robert Thomas and civic leaders Mayor Harold Thomas and George Griffiths, Chief Executive of Neath Borough Council.

NEATH RUGBY FOOTBALL CLUB

SEASON 1986/87   **CAPTAIN - JONATHAN DAVIES**

Sept.	1 North Wales XV	W	34	6	H
	6 Abertillery	W	50	6	A
	9 Cardigan	W	62	12	A
	13 Cardiff	W	24	7	H
	20 Newport	L	6	21	A
	27 Pontypridd	W	45	12	H
Oct.	4 Llanelli	W	11	10	H
	8 Newbridge	W	34	22	A
	11 Sale	W	15	9	A
	18 Swansea	W	22	10	A
	21 Ebbw Vale	W	20	10	H
	25 South Wales Police	W	30	17	H
Nov.	1 Pontypool	W	29	6	H
	8 Bridgend	W	13	8	A
	15 New Dock Stars (WRU Cup)	W	29	3	H
	22 Blackheath	L	9	21	A
	26 Maesteg	W	14	3	A
	29 Bath	W	26	9	H
Dec.	6 Orrell	L	7	15	A
	13 Bridgend	W	22	13	H
	20 Haverfordwest (WRU Cup)	W	41	3	H
	26 Aberavon	W	7	3	A
	27 Penarth	W	46	12	H
Jan.	1 Carmarthen Select	W	54	10	H
	3 Coventry	W	39	4	H
	6 South Glamorgan Institute	W	28	9	H
	10 Moseley	L	15	23	A
	24 Llanelli (WRU Cup)	W	15	3	H
	27 Newbridge	W	20	9	H
	3 Ebbw Vale	W	23	13	A
Feb.	14 Swansea	W	19	13	H
	18 Pontypridd	W	30	7	A
	21 Waterloo	L	20	24	A
	28 Pontypool (WRU Cup)	W	15	9	A
Mar.	3 South Wales Police	W	11	4	A
	9 Pontypool	W	16	15	A
	14 Maesteg	L	4	19	H
	16 Glamorgan Wanderers	W	29	13	A
	28 Cardiff (WRU Cup S/F at Swansea)	L	6	16	
Apr.	5 Richmond	W	42	25	H
	8 Cross Keys	W	38	7	A
	11 Gloucester	W	35	6	H
	18 Leicester	W	17	12	A
	20 Aberavon	W	48	10	H
	25 Cardiff	L	7	28	A

WELSH CHAMPIONS	*P*	*45*	
MERIT TABLE WINNERS	*W*	*37*	
ANGLO-WELSH PENNANT	*D*	*0*	
	L	*8*	
	F	*1107*	
	A	*517*	

Neath RFC's playing record in 1986/87.

	P	*W*	*D*	*L*	*F*	*A*	*%*
Neath (4)	37	30	0	7	869	451	81.08
Newport (5)	43	33	0	10	1083	657	76.74
Maesteg (12)	39	26	3	10	726	455	70.51
Cardiff (3)	39	25	2	12	941	656	66.66
Abertillery (19)	34	22	0	12	591	601	64.70
Brigend (11)	44	27	2	15	866	550	63.63
Llanelli (9)	41	24	2	15	895	640	60.97
Glamorgan W (2)	41	24	0	17	764	576	58.53
Swansea (7)	37	19	2	16	840	600	54.05
Pontypridd (17)	44	23	1	20	706	850	53.40
London Welsh (18)	33	17	0	16	553	746	51.51
S W Police (8)	38	19	1	18	741	591	51.31
Newbridge (13)	41	20	1	20	653	608	50.00
Pontypool (1)	43	21	0	22	776	718	48.83
Ebbw Vale (14)	40	19	0	21	693	682	47.50
Aberavon (6)	38	13	0	25	565	696	34.21
Penarth (15)	37	9	1	27	459	882	25.67
Tredegar (10)	33	7	2	24	337	601	24.24
Cross Keys (16)	36	2	0	34	257	1056	5.55

Those results were good enough to bring the Blacks their eighth Welsh championship and their third since the Second World War. Unusually, Neath's successes had come in 1946/47, 1966/67 and 1986/87 – but this time there would be no twenty-year wait until the next!

Above: The Neath championship-winning side of 1986/87, led by Jonathan Davies.

Right: Until the advent of Leagues and all the 'seriousness' they embraced, clubs supplied their own touch judges, except for WRU Cup finals and semi-finals. Neath's was Billy Thomas, a former WRU referee, who was a true all-year-round sportsman and spent his summers umpiring cricket for Neath 2nds.

Burly prop Stuart Evans was chosen to lead Neath in 1987/88. Although he first came to prominence with Swansea, whom he joined from British Steel Youth, Evans was very much a Neath man, having grown up in the town and played his junior rugby for Resolven. He joined his home town with Neath on the rise and soon established himself in the strongest pack in Wales, but left to join St Helen's RL in September 1987.

Neath played the USA on Saturday 31 October 1987, but were surprisingly beaten 6-15.

The programme from the 1987/88 Cup final, which was lost to Llanelli after Neath delayed the announcement of their team. Jonathan Davies had left Neath for the Scarlets and the star outside half turned the tables on his old club with a brilliant display of kicking which sapped the strength out of the Neath forwards.

UNDEB RYGBI CYMRU

WELSH RUGBY UNION

Schweppes Cup Final

LLANELLI

VERSUS

NEATH

Cardiff Arms Park   Saturday 7th May 1988

Ray Williams

Official Programme 60p   SECRETARY W.R.U

The final table from 1988/89.

WESTERN MAIL WELSH CLUBS CHAMPIONSHIP 1988-89

	P	W	D	L	F	A	%
Neath (2)	37	33	0	4	1423	384	89.18
Llanelli (4)	41	34	0	7	1260	670	82.92
Newbridge (11)	39	31	2	6	838	525	82.05
Bridgend (3)	43	32	0	11	904	583	74.41
Pontypridd (5)	38	27	1	10	1034	514	72.36
Swansea (7)	41	28	0	13	874	657	68.29
Cardiff (10)	36	19	4	13	780	694	58.33
Abertillery (6)	39	22	0	17	754	600	56.41
Maesteg (14)	42	22	3	17	732	695	55.95
Newport (16)	43	22	1	20	934	889	52.32
Ebbw Vale (9)	43	20	1	22	646	886	47.67
Pontypool (1)	41	18	0	23	706	805	43.90
Glam Wands (8)	40	17	1	22	760	696	43.75
S.W. Police (13)	38	13	1	24	650	741	35.52
Cross Keys (18)	37	11	2	24	449	874	32.43
Aberavon (12)	40	10	1	29	537	835	26.25
Tredegar (15)	36	9	0	27	430	873	25.00
London Welsh (17)	33	7	2	24	470	868	24.24
Penarth (19)	34	4	0	30	375	1124	11.76

Figures in brackets indicate finishing positions last season.

NEATH RUGBY FOOTBALL CLUB

SEASON 1988/89   **CAPTAIN : KEVIN PHILLIPS**

Sept.	3 Abertillery	W	15	-	10	A
	6 Briton Ferry	W	42	-	6	A
	10 Cardiff	W	49	-	10	H
	17 Newport	W	33	-	16	A
	20 O.G.Davies XV	W	47	-	6	H
	24 Pontypridd	W	14	-	10	H
Oct.	1 Llanelli	W	22	-	16	H
	7 Glamorgan Wanderers	W	27	-	13	A
	11 Abercrave	W	36	-	0	A
	15 Sale	W	48	-	17	A
	19 Ebbw Vale	W	50	-	0	A
	22 Swansea	L	19	-	20	A
	27 Stade Toulousaine	W	22	-	19	H
	29 Neath Athletic	W	40	-	13	H
Nov.	5 Pontypool	W	67	-	18	H
	14 Bridgend	W	22	-	3	A
	19 Caerphilly (WRU Cup)	W	46	-	0	H
	25 Cambridge University	W	38	-	6	H
Dec.	3 Orrell	W	22	-	13	A
	6 Llangennech	W	43	-	7	A
	12 Bridgend	W	49	-	0	H
	17 Abercarn (WRU Cup)	W	33	-	3	A
	21 Cross Keys	W	60	-	10	A
	26 Aberavon	W	34	-	10	A
	31 Neath Athletic	W	42	-	0	H
Jan.	2 Maesteg	W	32	-	6	A
	7 Ebbw Vale	W	58	-	3	H
	14 Llanelli	L	21	-	27	A
	22 London Welsh	W	48	-	15	H
	28 Blaina (WRU Cup)	W	47	-	12	H
Feb.	3 Greystones	W	66	-	19	H
	8 Newbridge	L	18	-	19	A
	11 Swansea	W	26	-	6	H
	15 Pontypridd	W	34	-	15	A
Mar.	4 Glamorgan Wanderers (WRU Cup)	W	38	-	0	A
	7 Newbridge	W	73	-	3	H
	11 Maesteg	W	64	-	0	H
	17 Wasps	W	34	-	4	H
	25 Coventry	W	42	-	9	A
	27 Aberavon	W	42	-	6	A
	29 Penarth	W	66	-	8	H
Apr.	1 Richmond	W	50	-	4	H
	8 Cardiff (WRU Cup S/F at Swansea)	W	19	-	12	
	12 Pontypool	W	33	-	9	A
	15 Cardiff	L	12	-	20	A
	19 Tredegar	W	44	-	7	H
	21 Dunvant	W	31	-	18	A
	24 South Wales Police	W	31	-	4	A
	29 Newport	W	54	-	7	H
May	6 Llanelli (WRU Cup Final at Cardiff)	W	14	-	13	

Played	50
Won	46
Drawn	0
Lost	4
Points For	1917
Points Against	472

Above: Neath RFC results, 1988/89.

Right: Hooker Kevin Phillips led Neath in 1988/89, 1989/90 and 1990/91. The Cardigan farmer epitomised the Neath 'up and at 'em' style. The sight of Kevin Phillips leading his troops from a quickly taken tap penalty into opposition ranks will remain in the memory forever. His leadership qualities transferred to the national XV, for whom he won 20 caps.

ten

Taking on
the World

Left: The programme from one of Neath's most memorable days. On 25 October 1989 Neath took on the might of New Zealand, winners of the first World Cup in 1987. Although Neath lost 15-26, they gave the tourists a mighty scare and, midway through the second half, there was only one point in it. Alan Edmunds got Neath's try and Paul Thorburn kicked 11 points. To mark the effort, a special booklet – 'One Day in October' – was produced by local journalist Rod Rees with photographs by Jim Giddings. The pair co-operated in producing the Neath programme at that time.

Below far left: As a result of an outstanding individual display in that game, back-row forward Phil Pugh was springboarded into the Wales team to play the tourists for his one and only cap. The Seven Sisters back-row man later returned as team manager in 1999.

Left: Allan Bateman was one of the classiest centres ever to play for Neath, and gave the scoring pass for Alan Edmunds' try against New Zealand. He later joined Warrington RL, played in Australia and was a double Union/League international. He returned to RU with Richmond and toured South Africa with the Lions in 1997, won the European Cup with Northampton and came back to Neath in 2001/02, ending his career with 35 RU caps.

Line-out action from the New Zealand game. Skipper Kevin Phillips prepares to throw in. The Neath players are Brian Williams, Mike Whitson, Jeremy Pugh, Gareth Llewellyn, Phil Pugh, Mark Jones and Martyn Morris. The imposing New Zealand line-out included Gary Whetton, Ian Jones and Zinzan Brooke.

Paul Thorburn prepares to convert Alan Edmunds' try.

Neath wasted no time in adding a tenth title in 1989/90 when they carried all before them, winning the *Western Mail* championship, the cup and the Merit Table. Their colours were lowered only by Bath, Llanelli and New Zealand, after which Neath won 37 consecutive games. Although playing two games less than in 1988/89, Neath scored 344 tries and 1,867 points with Paul Williams (282) and Paul Thorburn (236) the leading points scorers and Alan Edmunds (a post–war record of 45) and Rupert Moon (29) the leading try scorers.

WESTERN MAIL WELSH CLUBS CHAMPIONSHIP 1989-90

	P	W	D	L	F	A	%
Neath (1)	37	34	0	3	1377	347	91.89
Llanelli (2)	43	35	0	8	1249	675	81.39
Pontypool (12)	41	28	2	11	1071	565	70.73
Bridgend (4)	39	26	0	13	865	530	66.66
Glam Wands (13)	35	22	1	12	785	638	64.28
Swansea (6)	35	22	1	12	946	666	64.28
Newbridge (3)	38	24	0	14	852	525	63.15
Pontypridd (5)	37	21	0	16	929	639	56.75
Maesteg (9)	38	21	0	17	635	753	55.26
Cardiff (7)	40	19	2	19	904	761	50.00
Abertillery (8)	39	17	2	20	607	765	46.15
Cross Keys (15)	33	15	0	18	426	543	45.45
Ebbw Vale (11)	43	15	1	27	614	1012	36.04
Newport (10)	40	13	1	26	645	913	33.75
Ldn Welsh (18)	32	10	1	21	509	717	32.81
S W Police (14)	41	12	1	28	613	919	30.48
Aberavon (16)	39	9	0	30	484	849	23.07
Tredegar (17)	33	6	1	26	364	934	19.69
Penarth (19)	34	4	1	29	322	1370	13.23

Wing Alan Edmunds receives the Whitbread Player of the Month award for September 1990.

Above left: One of Neath's finest. Loose-head prop Brian Williams epitomised all that was best about Neath. The Pembrokeshire farmer joined Neath from Narberth in 1983/84 and, although considered by some to be 'too light', he had the raw strength to match anyone. He was everyone's hero in the magnificent Neath pack of the time and was capped by Wales 5 times from 1990. After almost severing his arm in a farming accident, it was feared that he would not play again, but back he came until retirement in 1995. He reappeared once for Neath as late as 1998/99.

Above centre: Pembrokeshire was a good nursery for Neath, and Welsh Schools' flanker Rowland Phillips of St David's made the leap. His intelligent footballing skills allied to a remarkable physical ability to stay on his feet soon brought him to the attention of the national selectors, and he won 10 caps before joining Warrington RL. He played international rugby league for Wales and, after spells back in Union with Treorchy and London Welsh, he rejoined Neath as captain in 1999/2000, and is now coach of the Welsh All Blacks.

Above right: Opposing packs crumbled before the fearsome Neath eight, and this often had much to do with having the not-inconsiderable physique of Mark Jones to contend with. The big No. 8 joined Neath from Tredegar in 1984/85, and was soon making an impression with his all-round power. After winning 14 caps, he too succumbed to the temptation of rugby league and joined Hull, before coming back to Wales with Ebbw Vale (where he earned a further cap) and later Pontypool, before rejoining Neath in 2003/04.

Opposite bottom: Neath beat Bridgend to win the cup in 1989/90. Lock Andrew Kembery was sent off by referee Clive Norling but the Blacks were good value for their 16-10 triumph. Pictured is the semi-final team. From left to right, standing: P. Pugh, H. Hughes (Physio), J. Ball, M. Morris, M. Jones, A. Kembery, G.O. Llewellyn, G.D. Llewellyn, B. Williams, C. Higgs, C .Laity, P. Thorburn, S. Webborn (Physio), D. Joseph, A. Thomas. Seated: J. Griffiths, C. Bridges, A. Edmunds, K. Phillips (Captain), P. Williams, R. Phillips, L. Jones, L. Isaac. Front: R. Moon, A. Bateman, A. Davies, J. Davies.

Paul Thorburn, as captain of Wales, introduces the Princess Royal to the Neath trio of Kevin Phillips, Glyn Llewellyn and Gareth Llewellyn prior to a Murrayfield international. The Llewellyns became the third pair of Neath brothers to represent Wales, following on from the Prossers (Glyn and Dai) and the Thomases (Dai Leysh and Harold) who appeared in the 1930s.

League rugby came to Wales in 1990/91. The first League game was against Abertillery on 22 September 1990 and full-back Paul Thorburn scored all Neath's points, including 2 tries, in a 16-9 win.

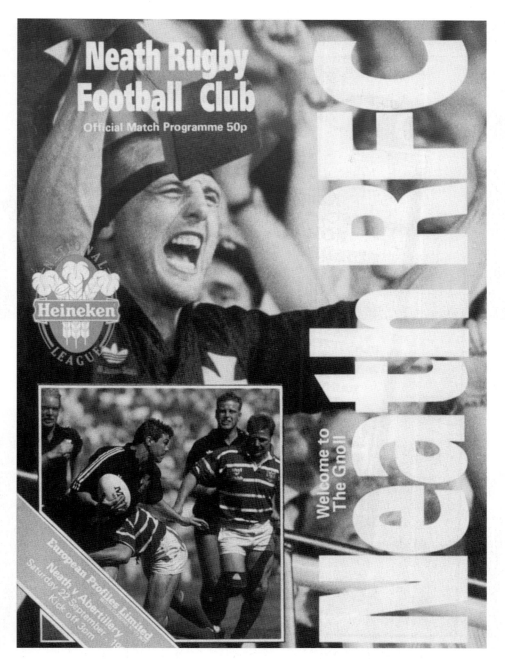

The programme from Neath's first-ever league game. Skipper Kevin Phillips proudly lifted the first Welsh League championship trophy at the end of the 1990/91 season, and Neath registered another first by becoming the inaugural champions, sewing up their eleventh title with some three rounds of fixtures remaining. This was the fourth season in five that Neath were Welsh champions – a remarkable record of consistency. In the year they missed out (1987/88) Neath finished runners-up to Pontypool.

On 11 November 1993 Neath lost to Australia 8-16, that outstanding prop Brian Williams bagging a try and Paul Thorburn kicking a penalty. Here Williams is supported by fellow forwards Kevin Phillips, John Davies and Glyn Llewellyn with Rhodri Jones, Lloyd Isaac, Jeff Bird and Martyn Morris in the background.

'Bag-snatchers!' That was the rather ungracious reaction from the Australian tourists (World Cup winners in 1991) when they too were exposed to The Gnoll challenge. The comment appears to have been directed at the style of tackling favoured by Neath, who had several farmers in the pack. Opposing forwards were picked up like sheep and dumped unceremoniously on the ground. Neath did not dignify the Aussie complaints with a response.

The President and Committee of the Welsh Rugby Union and Neath Rugby Football Club look forward to the pleasure of your company
at the

Celebration Dinner
in honour of the Australian Team

___

at the Glyn Clydach Hotel, Neath
Wednesday 11th November, 1992
5.30pm for 6pm

___

Dress : Lounge Suit/Blazer
Please produce this ticket on entrance

An invitation to the post-match dinner following the Neath *v*. Australia game.

Scrum-half Chris Bridges joined Neath from Beddau and won 7 caps for Wales in 1990 and 1991. He thus became Neath's first scrum-half to be capped since Eddie Watkins in 1924.

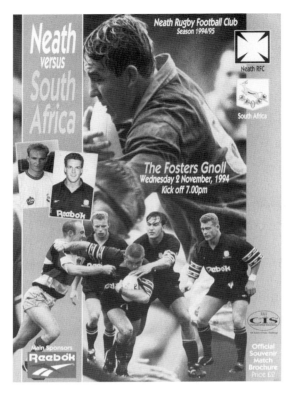

Left: In 1994/95, the game in Wales was still in name an amateur affair, but the return of South Africa to rugby's fold increased the pressure for professionalism. As a build-up to their hosting (and winning) the World Cup in 1995, the South Africans toured Wales and on 9 November 1994 Neath, as usual, met their challenge head-on. The Welsh All Blacks refused to be intimidated by the South Africans' physical approach and, putting up a tremendous fight, were mightily unlucky to lose 13–16.

Right: Neath celebrated their twelfth Welsh championship by winning the Premier Division in 1995/96. The side flourished after Christmas to register 9 consecutive League wins (including a 95-17 mauling of neighbours Aberavon) but they had to beat Pontypridd and score 7 tries in their final game to pip Cardiff to the title. No. 8 Steve Williams memorably gambolled away for that vital score and the champagne flowed as skipper Gareth Llewellyn collected the trophy.

Below near right: To succeed Kevin Phillips, Neath recruited hooker Barry Williams from Llandovery, and he was capped in 1996. He joined Richmond in May 1997, by which time he had been chosen for the British Lions tour to South Africa. After joining Bristol, he returned to Neath in 2002/03.

Far right: Gareth Llewellyn joined Neath from Llanharan in 1988/89 and, after starring against New Zealand for The Gnoll club, won his first cap against the tourists in 1989. He skippered Neath for four seasons from 1992/93 to 1995/96 before joining Harlequins, but returned in 2000/01 to lead for another three seasons. Prior to the 2003 World Cup, his cap tally was 79, a record for a Welsh forward.

	W	D	L	Bn	Tr	Pts
Neath	17	1	4	37	121	72
Cardiff	18	1	3	35	119	72
Pontypridd	16	1	5	28	98	61
Llanelli	15	0	7	29	88	59
Bridgend	12	1	9	22	73	47
Swansea	11	0	11	22	83	44
Ebbw Vale	11	0	11	8	44	30
Newport	10	1	11	9	43	30
Newbridge	9	0	13	11	47	29
Treorchy	5	1	16	10	45	21
Aberavon	3	0	19	8	38	14
Abertillery	2	0	20	8	43	12

Opposite below: The line-ups that contested the 'Battle of The Gnoll'. °Scrum-half Rhodri Jones scored a try for Neath, outside half Arwel Thomas converting and kicking 2 penalties. Both players came to Neath from Trebanos but both later transferred their allegiance to Swansea. In a tempestuous affair, prop Brian Williams was assaulted and concussed but played on. Neath matched fire with fire, yet the WRU, spurred on by the hysterical press response, launched an inquiry into the game. This rather irked Neath people, who considered that the WRU would have been better advised to investigate Swansea's alarming 72-7 defeat by the tourists. Again, Neath gave the world's best their closest and toughest match of their tour.

Neath RFC Committee 1995. From left to right, standing: M. Struel, D. Pickering, B. Allen, J. Williams, W. Thomas, R. Evans, R. Jenkins, C. Jones, A. Price, R. Rees. Seated: E. Case, D. Shaw, K. Davies, J. Prichard (Treasurer), B. Davies (Chairman), N. Rees, C. Niven, R. Williams, N. Biggs. Absent: A. Benjamin (Secretary).

Neath	CIS Co-operative insurance	Fiji
15 Geraint Davies	Full Back (Cefnwr)	Jonetani Waqa 15
14 Chris Higgs	Right Wing (Asgell dde)	Emori Bolobolo 14
13 Leigh Davies	Right Centre (Canolwr)	Lawrence Little 13
12 John Funnell	Left Centre (Canolwr)	Willie Rokotuiviwa 12
11 Richard Jones	Left Wing (Asgell chwith)	Manasa Bari 11
10 Paul Williams	Stand Off (Maswr)	Opeti Turuva 10
9 Patrick Horgan	Scrum Half (Mewnwr)	Sekoue Rauluni 9
1 Darren Morris	Loose Head Prop (Y rheng flaen)	Sekoue Sadria 1
2 Kevin Allen	Hooker (Bachwr)	Greg Smith 2
3 John Davies *	Tight Head Prop (Y rheng flaen)	Viliame Cavubati 3
4 Glyn Llewellyn *	Lock (Yr ail reng)	Aiskae Nadolo 4
5 Gareth Llewellyn * (Capt)	Lock (Yr ail reng)	Leveni Vatureba 5
6 Justin Burnell	Left Flanker (Blaenasgell)	Waisiki Masirewa 6
8 Steve Williams *	No.8 (Y rheng ol)	Sakeasi Vonolagi (Capt) 8
7 Chris Scott	Right Flanker (Blaenasgell)	Emori Katalau 7

Chris McDonald, Mike Morgan,
Chris Beukes, Robin Jones,
Huw Woodland †, Martyn Morris *

Jason McClennan, Rasolosolo Bogisa,
Phillipe Raysi, Paula Bale,
Eminomi Batimala, Joeli Veitayaki

* Full Internationals † 'B' Internationals

Today's Officials

Referee Mr Ed Morrison R.F.U.
Touch Judge No.1 Mr. Jerry Wallis R.F.U.
Touch Judge No.2 Mr. Chris White R.F.U.
Rep. Touch Judge Mr. Clayton Thomas W.R.U.

NEATH RFC

The Welsh Rugby Union and Neath RFC ask spectators not to run on to the field of play during half time.
Anyone who does so may be removed from the ground. We thank you for your co-operation

FIJI RFU

On 25 October 1995, Neath defeated Fiji 30-22 through tries by Chris Higgs, Leigh Davies, John Funnell and Chris Scott and 10 points from the boot of Paul Williams.

Neath RFC 1995/96 – Wales' first champions of the professional era. From left to right, back row:
J.D. Davies, C. Bridges, I. Boobyer, H. Woodland, K. Allen, L. Gerrard, M. Morgan. Standing:
D. Case, C. Beukes, Robin Jones, G.D. Llewellyn, A. Kembery, M. Morris, J. Burnell. Seated:
L. Davies, B.H. Williams, P. Thorburn, G.O. Llewellyn (Captain), S. Williams, John Funnell,
C. Higgs, P. Williams. Front: P. Horgan. D. Morris, Joe Funnell, R. Wintle, G. Evans, G. Davies.
Absent: C. Scott, Richard Jones.

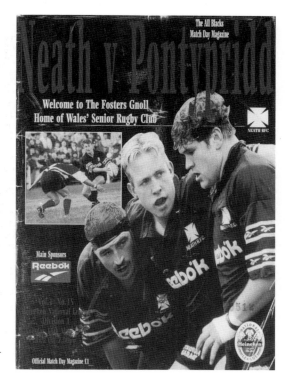

The programme from Neath *v.* Pontypridd –
the night Neath won the title.

Postscript

Rugby went professional on that fateful Sunday morning in August 1995, and it is fair to say that the ramifications are still being felt in Welsh rugby. For Wales' oldest senior club, 'going pro' was a chastening experience, not least in financial terms. The professional era has not been easy for a club that always placed greater emphasis on personal pride and collective passion than on any material benefits that might accrue to individuals from the game.

However, the Welsh All Blacks adjusted to the times and Neath rugby has prevailed. In 2002/03 – the last season of professional club rugby in Wales – Neath finished a creditable second in the Welsh League and became the only club side ever to reach the final of the Celtic Cup. That worthy tournament will henceforth be the pursuit of provincial sides as Welsh rugby embarks upon a new 'regional' future.

But Neath RFC is still alive and kicking in the Welsh Premier League. Those who served the All Black cause so loyally over the past 130-plus years, whether on the field as players or off the field as administrators and supporters, will rejoice in the continuation of a legend. Indeed, they would have it no other way!

Opposite: G.O. (Gareth) Llewellyn, Neath RFC captain for seven seasons (1993 to 1996 and 2000 to 2003) and Wales' most-capped forward.

Other local titles published by Tempus

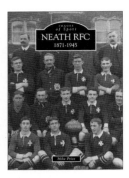

Neath RFC 1871-1945

MIKE PRICE

One of the most famous names in Welsh rugby is that of Neath Rugby Football Club. Neath RFC is also the most senior and, from their early beginnings in 1871/72, the Welsh All Blacks have enjoyed a rich, sometimes tragic, history. Neath secretary Mike Price has brought some of that proud history back to life with a blend of team photographs, player portraits and other printed memorabilia.

0 7524 2709 1

Swansea RFC 1873-1945

BLEDDYN HOPKINS

The 'All Whites' were founded in 1873 and became one of the eleven founder clubs of the Welsh Rugby Union in 1881. Swansea Rugby Club's history is renowned the world over for its many achievements. This volume traces the club's development from its formation through to the end of the Second World War. It gives a fascinating insight into the club and features team photographs, player portraits, action shots and many items of club memorabilia.

0 7524 2721 0

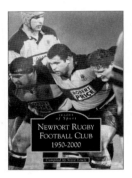

Newport Rugby Football Club 1950-2000

STEVE LEWIS

Continuing the story of Newport Rugby Football Club, this collection of over 200 images and accompanying text commences in 1950 and brings the story of this famous club into the twenty-first century. Essential reading for followers of Newport Rugby Football Club and supporters of the game everywhere, this book brings to a close the 125-year story of one of the game's most famous clubs.

0 7524 2084 4

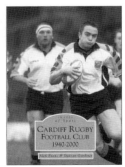

Cardiff Rugby Football Club 1940-2000

ALAN EVANS & DUNCAN GARDINER

The rich history of Cardiff Rugby Football Club is vividly brought to life in this superb book. Over sixty years of history is covered, including the time a bomb fell on Cardiff Arms Park in 1941, victories over the All Blacks and Wallabies, the centenary year, some astonishing cup wins during the 1980s and the pursuit of glory in Europe in recent times.

0 7524 2181 6

If you are interested in purchasing other books published by Tempus, or in case you have difficulty finding any Tempus books in your local bookshop, you can also place orders directly through our website

www.tempus-publishing.com

or from **BOOKPOST**, Freepost, PO Box 29, Douglas, Isle of Man, IM99 1BQ
tel 01624 836000   email bookshop@enterprise.net